ME JEWEL
AND DARLIN'
DUBLIN

First published in 1974
Second edition (revised) 1975
Third edition 1977

The O'Brien Press,
11 Clare Street Dublin 2 Ireland
ISBN 0 905140 27 3

Printed in Ireland by
E. & T. O'Brien Ltd., Dublin.

Me jewel and darlin' Dublin

by Eamonn Mac Thomáis

for Melíosa my daughter

Illustrated by Michael O'Brien

THE O'BRIEN PRESS

11 Clare Street Dublin 2 Ireland

Contents

HIDDEN PLACES

THE CITY CENTRE

Children at play in the Liberties. Grey Street looking towards Meath Street.

Illustrations

Below is a list of illustrations in page order. The source is stated in each case where this is possible. Generally where no acknowledgement or source is stated the illustration is a drawing by Michael O'Brien. We would like to thank all those who helped with the supply of illustrated material.

About this book

The history of Dublin is so vast that it is only possible to present in a book of this size a taste of what lies underneath. Nevertheless, what we present is a Dubliner's Dublin, written, illustrated and published by Dubliners. The author has spent thirty years studying his city and has waded through dozens and dozens of books, maps and pamphlets in the many libraries and institutions that house this great store of knowledge. Essentially the many tales and recollections are told in the authentic Dublin manner, and we hope the reader will appreciate and enjoy this flavour.

The author and publishers wish to thank all those listed below who in one way or another helped to make this book possible.

A special thanks to Mr. F. E. Dixon for help in many ways, the staff of The National Library, Marsh's Library, The Royal Irish Academy and the Dublin City Libraries—Pearse Street, Kevin Street, Emmet Road and Rathmines. Also Radio Eireann, especially the 'Morning Airs' staff who helped with the 'Discover Dublin' series, and Dublin Tourism.

Thanks also to John G. Rathborne Ltd., Thomas Read & Co. Ltd., Arthur Guinness Son & Co. Ltd., Brian Byrne of the Hideout Kilcullen, Maureen Potter, Elgy Gillespie, the Pembrey family of Green 's Bookshop, Roisin MacThomais, Colm Henry, Olwyn Callaghan, Nuala Gunn, Peggy Ashe and Valerie O'Brien.

The following deserve our thanks also — An Daonscoil, The Old Dublin Society, The Liberties Association, The Republican Movement, The Robert Emmet Society, Dean of St. Patrick's, Inchicore and District Historical Society, Irish Georgian Society, The Dublin Arts Festival, and The Royal Society of Antiquaries of Ireland.

A Childs World

The Fourpenny Rush

First it was the Twopenny Rush, then the Threepenny Rush and when they got the Picture House painted, and new Woodeners and Cushioners installed it went up to the Fourpenny Rush.

My friend Bonker said "that the price now was universal", "what does that mean?", we asked. "All over the world" said Bonker "it's fourpence everywhere, it's something got to do with the union". But we were never able to figure out what the South Dublin Union, and the stiffs in the Morgue had to do with the price of the pictures on a Saturday or Sunday afternoon.

The Fourpenny Rush in the local cinemas kept the kids off the streets. It taught them what they never learned in school, it was a college in memory training, because every kid could tell you, line for line and act for act, all about the Big Picture or the Folly-in-Upper (serial picture).

An hour before the show started a queue would form up. The ushers would beat the children back with leather belts "Keep in line, keep in line" they shouted as the sweat rolled off their brows. It was quite an effort trying to handle a thousand children pushing and shoving, pulling pigtails, throwing orange peels and clutching dearly to the four pennies admission fee.

Bonker was right, it was fourpence everywhere as we toured the local cinemas of Dublin. They were, the 'Core' at Inchicore, the 'Ri' (Rialto), and the Leinster at Dolphin's Barn, 'The Fountain' in James's Street, 'The Tivo' in Francis Street, 'The Mayro' in Mary Street, 'The Phoeno' on the quays, and 'The Broad' in Manor Street. Most of these cinemas have since been closed.

Sometimes we went into town to The Pillar Cinema or The Grand Central in O'Connell Street, or around to The Masterpiece or The New Electric in Talbot Street, or perhaps The Camden or 'The Lux' (De-Luxe) in Camden Street or The Green in Stephen's Green. Now and then we ventured out as far as the Stella and the 'Prinner' (Princess) on the Rathmines Road nearly facing 'Homeville' where I was born. It was shanks mare (walking) there and back from our homes in Kilmainham. If we had a penny to spend the last thing we'd spend it on was a tram or a bus, wet or fine we walked everywhere.

The Hero in the Picture was known as 'the Chap', his girlfriend as 'the Mot', the Chap also had a Pal, and a dog or a horse which could do tricks. They all got a roaring standing ovation, while the Head Crook, his Mot and the other crooks all got a hiss and a boo. We hated Love Pictures, but liked Gene Autry, Tom Mix, Roy Rogers, Buck Jones and Tarzan the best, because they never kissed girls. No matter how tough the fight, Gene Autry never lost his hat — and he could kill twelve Indians with one shot out of his gun.

Best for laughs were Wheeler and Wolsey, Charlie Chaplin, The Keystone Cops, Pop-Eye and his girlfriend Olive Oil, and Laurel and Hardy ("This is another nice mess you got me into Stanley"). Although we hated girls Shirley Temple was different and we all saw "The Little Princess" three times. Dublin had its own Shirley Temple contest, and a little girl from the road where I lived was in the first ten.

The outstanding greats of those days were 'Boys' Town', Mickey Rooney, Spencer Tracey, The Dead End Kids in 'Angels with Dirty Faces', James Cagney and 'The Roaring Twenties', 'The Bolero' with George Raft, 'Northwest Passage', 'Mr. Stanley and Dr. Livingstone', 'Jesse James', 'The Daltons Rode Again' and 'Charlie Chan'. We also loved Peter Lorre in detective pictures 'Murder at the Wax Museum' and the wonderful singing pictures of Nelson Eddy and Jeanette McDonald.

The local cinema was more than a picture house, it was a community centre, a place to kill a few hours, something to look forward to, a chance for your mother to wear her new hat, a university of conversation, because who-ever saw the picture first would come home and tell the whole road about it.

The Tivoli Cinema, Francis Street, currently in use as a Bingo Hall

Television is killing the local cinema and it is also helping to kill conversation. Practically everyone will have seen a picture shown on telly, because everyone has a telly, but the local cinema was different. Each cinema had two, sometimes three different shows per week. If you missed the picture on Monday you made sure that you saw it on Tuesday or Wednesday. No matter how good the telly is it's not a night out for the woman or man of the house. Men and women, boys and girls could see a three-hour show sitting on the Woodeners for fourpence.

At one stage several cinemas took jam jars instead of cash. That happened in the Twopenny Rush days. If you handed in a threepenny bit you might be stuck with two one pound jam jars for your change. Can you imagine sitting on the woodeners, trying to balance two jam jars, peel your orange, and keep your eye on the Chap, the Mot and the Crook — or worry yourself sick in case Stanley might not be able to find Dr. Livingstone in the jungle.

As my friend would say "To think that he could find him in a jungle like that, and we got lost on the way home from the Roxy last Sunday". The Roxy later became the Rotunda Cinema and is now The Ambassador.

I knew a man who could neither read nor write, yet never missed a picture at his local cinema. He was a gifted storyteller and had the greatest memory in all Kilmainham. One day I said to him, "You are a remarkable man, I wonder what you would be to-day if you could read and write!" He laughed and said "I never missed the books and the pens, and sure there's only bad news in the newspapers, I learned all I ever wanted to know at the Fourpenny Rush in The Tivo — and do you see them Pullman seats to-day at a £1 a go — well they could not carry drinks nor hold a candle to the woodeners in the old Fourpenny Rush".

A Dublin Penny

One of the many types of pennies
used in Dublin over the centuries
George IV Copper Penny of 1823

"Did you see him Mary?" my mother would say, "Did you see him looking up into their faces for a penny?" Whenever we stopped to talk to people on the street I was always accused and bashed for looking up into their faces for a penny.

A penny was a lot of money in those days. With it you could buy the evening newspaper, weigh yourself, take a tram ride from Inchicore to College Green, or buy a dinner for a poor man at the Little Flower Hall in the Liberties. A penny would buy a small bottle of milk, or a large bag of broken biscuits from the Kingdom Stores in James's Street, a quarter of a pound of fat rashers (for a coddle), 2 ozs. of Maggie Ryan (Margarine), a penny pot of jam, or a large slice of Miss Noone's Gur Cake (Fruit Cake) hot from the oven, or two coffin nails (cigarettes) and a few matches.

It would also buy a small packet of Lyons Tea, a ball of blue, a tin of polish, a packet of Drummer Dye, a pair of boot laces, a seat on the fancy toilet in the Metropole, or a box of Beecham's Pills which the David Allen Bill Boards said were worth a guinea a box. Perhaps for your penny you would like a white clay pipe which you didn't have to pick up if it fell, a split loaf (cat's lick and all), a large turnip, four onions, or a pint of paraffin oil, for the Sacred Heart lamp.

For the same penny you could have a half a stone of logs, a little coal, or a hot buttered egg from the Monument Creamery. A really special treat was a penny ice cream wafer in Coppolo's of Cuffe Street, which one would still be sucking at Rialto Bridge. A variety of sweets were available for the same penny, 12 Rainbow Caramels, 32 Aniseed Balls, 16 Jembo Balls, 2 Peggies Legs, or 2 Lucky Bags. You might prefer a pear, an apple, an orange, or two 'Taffey' apples, a fishing net, or two black babies — they were a halfpenny each. I can remember being sent home from school to get the halfpenny for the black babies which I forgot to bring with me that morning. Despite all the money I gave to the nuns and masters I never saw any results, and was always bitterly disappointed that they never brought in my black babies.

A penny would take you into Mass on a Sunday by the back door, (the front door was threepence). It would light a candle, buy a holy picture, or could be presented to the poor woman with the child in her arms, sitting outside the church door. There were three types of Dublin Pennies: the black Victorian type, the brown Edwardian type, and the Golden Hen with a harp

Left – Tossing for it along the Quays. Above (1) Hiberno-Norse Silver Penny struck in Dublin about 1000 – 1010 A.D. (2) Edward I Silver Penny struck in Dublin 1280. (3) The once familiar Victorian Bronze Penny. (4) The 'golden hen' Irish Penny commonly used until replaced by decimal coins recently. A long line of pennies all used in Dublin.

on the other side. When my uncle came to visit, he always gave me a brand new Golden Hen. With a bit of skill the new penny could be transformed into a Half Crown, and if I got a chance I would change it in Muldowney's Pub.

A story is told of a Dublin man who saw a large bottle of Gold Label Whiskey in a public house and on its price tag was marked 'One Penny'. He ordered the bottle, but the publican explained that a mistake had been made, that the price was really 'one pound'. With that a policeman came into the pub, heard the story, and told the publican, 'The Law says you must sell the bottle for a penny'. The lucky man then left the shop with the bottle. A few days later the policeman met the man in the street. He laughed and said 'Be the hokey I'll never forget the look on the publican's face when I told him he would have to give you the big bottle of whiskey for a penny'. The man laughed and said 'You should have seen the look on his face when I went back the next day for a penny on the empty bottle'.

Street Games

"All in, all in, the game is broke up. All in, all in, the game is broke up". Someone wasn't playing the game (Re-Leave-Eio); at least he wasn't playing it according to the Rowserstown rule book, so the words rang out in the night, like the old town criers, "All in, all in, the game is broke up" — You could hear it a half a mile away. It always seemed to come just as you had found a good hiding place in the Robbers Den, or across the Camac River near the old mill.

After the 'All in' sound we would come back to the street lamp near the steps to the high road — the flies and moths playing their own chasing game around the bright glow of the old gas lamp. "What is it now, who broke up the game, tell me who it was and I'll burst him. Let's play another game, let's go home, let's start a fire, let's box the fox in the seven orchards. Let's go up to Goldenbridge and play 'Mind the Thread' ".

"You-a, you-a all the gang. You-a, you-a all the gang, don't forget your hoops" (a bicycle wheel without spokes or tyre, and a piece of stick to beat the hoop along). Within seconds fourteen hoops would be belting up Rowserstown and down to Kilmainham cross-roads. There were no traffic lights in those days, and if you stopped to let a tram pass, you were chicken.

Now for 'Mind the Thread'. "Who's going to be on it? — ok you two". Two boys, one at each side of the path, would sit on the ground pretending to be holding a piece of thread between them. It was held about six inches off the ground. The game would suddenly start as a man or woman came walking up the path. As soon as they came quite near, one of the boys would start shouting 'Mrs., Mrs., mind the thread'. The poor woman thinks there's a thread on the ground so she starts lifting her legs, jumping and dancing to avoid the

14

thread. 'Ah Mrs. Mrs. don't Mrs.' — that really had her hopping and we all sitting on the far side of the road, holding our sides with the laughter. Of course some people knew we had no thread, and entered into the game for fun. I played it a thousand times and I never remember anyone getting cross or cranky. Some were even surprised they could hop so high. If they had a sour face coming to the thread they usually had a smile and a laugh leaving it.

'Follow the Leader' was a dangerous game, particularly if you were at the end of the line. The leader started off and we had to follow in single file. Anything the leader did the rest behind had to do also; knocking on doors, ringing bells, rattling ash-bin lids. By the time the last few got to the door or ash-bin, the owner was on the scene and all those at the end of the line ended up with a few clouts on the ear or a kick in the backside.

'Kick the Can' was another favourite. I think this was invented for those who couldn't afford a football. The boy 'on it' stood by the can, and we had to kick the can without the boy 'on it' touching us. A lot of skill was required, because some boys nearly sat on the can — nevertheless the can was often kicked up and down the road. The game usually ended with a good chase from Mr. Kearney, who always threatened to get the Po-liss. Poor Mr. Kearney, he never had a dull evening.

We used to play another game called 'Rope the Door'. We would tie a rope to the door knob and pull hard, then someone would knock on the door. Inside poor Mr. Kearney would be trying to open the door *in,* and at the same time we would pull the door *out.* The tug-o'-war would go on for about five minutes, then Mr. Kearney would slip out the back-door, wearing a pair of white runners and the Goldenbridge Steeplechase would begin. In later years, Mr. Kearney told me that while he was mad with rage at the start of the chase, he was always in great form at the end of it. He was surprised that he could run so fast (he often caught a few of us), and it also helped to keep his weight down.

Whips and Wooden Tops, Taw in the Hole (marbles played like golf), Kattie, Combo Round Towers, Hide and Seek, Tip and Tig, Blind Man's Buff, Hurling and Football were all played on the road until you heard 'L.O.B., L.O.B. — Look Out Boys it's the cops'. Some children called them police, others called them cops, peelers, rawsers, or po-liss. The local sergeant often arrived on his upstairs model of a bicycle with its weak carbine lamp. The L.O.B. rarely failed, and even if it did, there was always plenty of time to get away. The sergeant took about ten minutes to get down off his bicycle, take the bicycle clips off his trousers and put out his carbine lamp, before proceeding with his notebook and pencil.

Card Playing was another favourite. A game of Rummy, Pontoon, 15's, 25's, Snap, Old Maid, Dawn and Solo. Of these Dawn was the most popular. It was played like this — the nine of Trumps was known as Big Fat, and the five of Trumps as Little Fat. You played it with partners like Whist. If you wanted your partner to head with a certain suit of cards you would work the tip-off system: ·Spades — "I saw your father digging the garden to-day". Diamonds — "Mary Murphy's getting married, her fella gave her a lovely ring". Clubs — start singing 'The Dear Little Shamrock, The Sweet Little Shamrock'. Hearts — Putting your hand on your chest and saying, 'I've got an awful pain there'. Pretty primitive stuff, but its surprising how it worked.

My favourite game was Pitch and Toss or 'Up to the Mottie', which was another form of Pitch and Toss. Morning, noon and night I would play Pitch and Toss. I really loved it, until the man next door told my mother that he saw me playing it, and that it was a very common game, as common as ditchwater, he said (a terrible insult) and she should make me give it up. A common game? If I'd known that night what I know now — far from being a common game, it was in fact a Royal game. It was started by King Edward III, and the piece of stick used to balance the two coins on got its name from Edward. They say this King got very angry when he lost at Pitch and Toss, and he used to throw down the tossing stick and say 'Feck it Feck it' — thereafter the tossing stick became known as the Feck, and its still called that. You put the two halfpennies on to the feck and toss them into the air — Heads you win — Harps or Tails you lose.

An American visitor once said that the Dublin people were the holiest people in the world. "How come?" asked his friend "Well," said the American "at every street corner in Dublin the men stand around in circles, they all look up to Heaven and bow down their heads to the ground and shout out — 'Good Christ, show us a head this time'." Pitch and Toss was not only a child's game, but was, and still is a man's game. At the big Pitch and Toss school in the brickfields I saw a man lose all his money, and also his pony and trap, and he had to go home on the crossbar of a friend's bicycle.

'Up to the Mottie' was another game. Our mottie was a small square piece of white broken delph stuck into the black clay on the side paths. When the Corpo (Dublin Corporation) put concrete over this clay patch we then changed the game to 'Up to the Wall'. You only needed a halfpenny to enter the game, pitch it to the path wall, the nearest halfpenny to the wall was the winner and he also got the first chance to toss the halfpennies for the next round.

After every wedding, well *almost* every wedding in our local church, the groom or best man would 'Grush the Money'. As the newly-weds were about to drive off, the shouts went up "Mister, Mister, grush the money — grush the money", and a paper bag of pennies, halfpennies, threepenny bits and a few odd sixpence pieces would sail into the air and crash down in all directions, jingling and rolling. If you were lucky, you'd get a few pence or maybe a six-pence piece. If you were unlucky you'd get a kick on the ear, and a black eye. The wedding of the year was judged by the size of the grush. With a penny grush money and a lucky game of pitch and toss you would have the price of the pictures and a few pence to spend, or could participate in another game of pitch and toss the following day.

16

Sometimes we played the girls' games of Skipping, Swinging on a Rope tied to a Lamp Post or Piggie Beds and Shop. We always backed out when the games changed to 'School', or 'House' (Mammies & Daddies). 'Piggie Beds' was played on the paths with square or round rings marked out with chalk — the 'Beds' were like a ladder and you tipped the 'Piggie' (a shoe-polish box filled with clay) and it slid from Bed to Bed — if it went into the wrong Bed or onto the chalk line of the Bed you were out of the game. As you tipped the Piggie with one foot, you hopped along at the same time. This really was a game of skill as you had to balance on one foot, tip the Piggie with it and hop from Bed to Bed.

'Shop' was played with "Chaney Money". 'Chanies' were pieces of broken delph, small — about the size of a new Half Penny — the more colourful the piece of chaney, the better it was, as you could buy more with a few coloured pieces than you could with a few white pieces.

The contents of the 'Shop' consisted of Dog or Dock Leaves (very good for cooling your hand if you get the sting of a nettle). Dandelion leaves were also for sale. We dried them in the sun, allowed them to rot, and used them in clay pipes for tobacco. Other items were empty boxes, an odd jam jar, comics and cigarette pictures.

At that time cigarette pictures were all the rage — they came free with every packet of cigarettes and were very colourful and educational. They came in series and a full set could be exchanged for gifts — Wills Goldflake gave little playing cards, and Carrolls gave Sweet Afton Coupons. For hours we would stand at Kilmainham Cross or at Sarah Bridge, "Mister, any cigarette pictures, please" — our pockets would be bulging with all sorts of pictures. We never got any gifts for them, but we got hours of pleasure. We swopped them for comics, sweets, a cigarette butt, a look at your Mickey Mouse Watch. "A go on a gig" cost 50 cigarette pictures. The 'gig' was a flat board on four ball races (wheels) with a piece of strong twine for steering tied to the front axle. As you sat on the gig, your pal pushed your back — going down hills it was all free-wheel.

We must not forget 'Cowboys and Indians', and 'Cops and Robbers'. They are both still favourites today. Strange how everyone wanted to be a Robber. Another game, and one I hated, yet played because I didn't want to be chicken — "Come on will ya, come on will ya, we're going to have a look at the stiffs". Down to the Union Morgue we would go and in around the slabs, where sixteen or seventeen bodies were awaiting burial. Some with pennies on their eyes and big bluebottles (flies) in their hundreds flying around like jet aeroplanes, landing now and again on the face of a corpse. I'd be shaking like a leaf as we crept around the bodies, the silence broken only by the buzzing of bluebottles — then someone would shout out "He moved, he moved" and without waiting to find out who had moved we would scatter for the door, and not even Mick the Miller, the famous greyhound, could catch us.

The Old Ways

The Pawnshops of Dublin

The early Monday morning tram was crowded. It was the same every Monday morning, not a seat or space to spare. Packed like a tin of sardines, the luggage bay was full of clothes, suits, blankets, shoes, and a set of aluminium saucepans. Downstairs one woman sat beside St. Joseph, another woman had the Child of Prague on her lap. Two eight-day clocks, each with a different time took up two other seats. Upstairs, as usual, The Sacred Heart was in the front seat with a glass shade around him. He stood three feet tall, beside a big fat woman, who had one arm on the seat and the other around The Sacred Heart.

When the tram stopped at The Fountain in James's Street nearly every-one got off. First came the saucepans, and the clothes, then St. Joseph, and someone stood back to let the woman with the 'Child' descend. The last to leave were the Sacred Heart, followed by the two clocks. The procession proceeded to cross the street. At the sign of the three brass balls and the name Patrick Gorman, 31 James's Street, Pawnbroker, the procession ended as it moved up the lane to The Counter Door. The inside of the shop was a hive of activity. "Ask for six and take four, wan gent's suit navy blue eight shillings, set of saucepans three shillings, the coat pocket is torn mam, St. Joseph again four shillings, the Child again two and six. Here's yer ticket, yer ticket, are ye deaf?" — "Give us six Tom on the coat, it's a crombie". "I'll give ya four, the pocket is torn". "Ah go' man Tom, six shillings". "Four is all it's worth" — "Well give us five". "Four and six is as far as I go". "You're terrible mean Tom, make it five shillings..". "Seven and sixpence the Sacred Heart in a glass shade." — "Four and six for the coat. Here's your ticket." "Only four and six for a Crombie, I'll be kilt when I go home."

The sign of the three brass balls is almost a thing of the past. In 1838 there were 700 pawn shops in Ireland and fifty seven in Dublin. One hundred years later there were still forty or more in Dublin. There were three pawn shops in Summerhill, two in Gardiner Street, and one in the following north-side streets: Amiens, Talbot, Parnell, Granby Row and Capel Street, Ellis Quay, Queen Street, Dominick Street, Dorset Street and two in Marlborough Street.

On the south side of the Liffey there were two in Cuffe Street, Charlemont Mall, and one in James's Street, Bishop Street, Richmond Street, Bride Street, Clanbrassil Street, Francis Street, the Coombe, Ardee Street and Winetavern Street. Others were located in Fleet Street, Erne Street, Lombard

Street, Baggot Street, Mount Street, Ringsend, and at Nineteen-and-a-Half Main Street Blackrock, and two in Lower George's Street, Dunlaoghaire. All were under private names with the exception of the one in Number Seven Buckingham Street, which was registered as 'The Great Northern Pawn Office'.

The first things people pawned were their own clothes, coats, dresses, suits, hats, etc. As they got poorer they pawned the clothes off the bed; as they continued to get poorer they pawned religious pictures, statues, clocks, pots, pans, patriotic pictures, and when they were the poorest of the poor they pawned the chair they sat on. The pawnbroker did not make money on the objects pawned, even if the objects were never redeemed. He made his money on the number of pledges (items pawned). The pawnbroker had a fixed levy on each pawn ticket and due to the thousands of tickets issued the profits rolled in. The pawn office was open from early morning until 10.30 p.m. Monday to Saturday. The pawnbrokers' tickets stated "Fine Airy Wardrobes for your Clothes". The fine airy wardrobes were dozens of six inch nails stuck into a wooden wall.

Some people didn't give a damn being seen going to the pawn, others tried to slip in and out unnoticed. From Trinity College students came with camel hair coats, college books, Boswells Life of Johnston , Gulliver's Travels , gold watches and straw hats. Others came with saucepans with no lids, broken shoes, torn coats, religious statues, ponies and carts, bicycles and suites of furniture, and gold wedding rings. The pawn was the place to go, make

John Brereton of Capel Street, still in business with the familiar sign.

your pledge, get your ticket, redeem the article the following Saturday and pledge it back in the following Monday. Year in, year out, the pawn was a way of life. It put bread on many a poor man's table or saved a college student from being evicted out of his Rathmines flat.

The Pawnbrokers' Assistants were a very respectable class of gentlemen, at one time they had to live-in and were not allowed to get married until they served their seven years' apprenticeship. Many got married before the allowed time and had to go to bed with their wives on their dinner hour. I knew one assistant who changed his clothes everyday. He had to, his mother wouldn't let him in, "Take off your flea suit before you come in here," she'd say as she threw another suit out the kitchen window — poor John, he's dead now, changed in a shed in the back garden.

Tommy Armstrong was another character who had a pawn shop in Ardee Street. He always tied his trousers at the knees, to keep the fleas out. Around this time Singer Sewing Machines were being sold door-to-door at a shilling per week. One day a man stuck his head into Tommy's pawn shop and said, "Mister A, Mister A, would you be interested in a Singer Sewing Machine" — "'Deed and I wouldn't" said Tommy, "Sure every arsehole in Dublin has wan of them." Tommy followed a long line of tradition in the pawnbroking business.

If a rich man wanted money he took the deed of his house or land to the Bank, arranged a loan, and that was a business transaction and he was a business man. If a poor woman wanted bread for her children she took the clothes off the bed, went to the pawn, made a pledge, and she was a pauper.

Soon to go for road-widening, Gorman's Pawnbrokers 'Late of Winetavern Street' and The Bricklayers Hall in Cuffe Street (see St. Stephen's Green chapter).

The three brass balls go back to the house of Lombard, the traditional gold plate sign later became a ball, and then two others were added for effect. 'The Lombards' was a term used for the merchants, goldsmiths and money-lenders who came from Genoa, Florence, and Venice, which could account for the three balls, one for each city. The Lombards gave us our commercial terms which we use every day:- debtor, creditor, cash, bank, journal, diary, ditto, and the old £ s. d. (before D. Day) which originally stood for Libri Soldi, Denarii. The Lombards granted the first loan to the States and took the customs (from imports) as their pledges.

The first pawn shop was set up in Rome by The Emperor Augustus. When he fed people to the lions in the Coliseum he took over their property and used it to grant small loans. In the fifteenth century a Franciscan priest set up a pawn shop in Assisi. His was a special type known as The House of Mont-de-Piete. Germany and Italy followed suit, and King Billy (William of Orange) organised one in Holland.

The oldest pawn record in the National Library, is a letter to Col. J. Fitzsimmons, Roscommon, dated February 1664, concerning the redeeming of the waistcoat of Sir James Dillon which was pawned for £10 by Lady Dillon. In 1634 the Dublin Corporation pawned The City Seal for £1,000.

"Ask for six and take four", "I don't care if you're kilt". Today pawnbroking continues, and so do the pawn office auction sales, you'll see them advertised in the small ad. columns of the evening papers. The next time you see three brass balls you'll know the sign doesn't mean "Two to wan, you won't get it back".

Some recent auction advertisements
from pawnbrokers

DUBLIN PAWNSHOP

Three brass balls
Four black shawls
A clock, St. Anthony
Robert Emmet
A willow delph.
Another shawl
With bedclothes.
A man with two suits
Scholars with University books.
A plumber with a bicycle,
A jarvey with no horse –
All pledged and lodged
For bread, rent
And drink.
One and nine
That's it
Give us two bob,
He'll have a fit
One and nine
Its a torn quilt
The devil take ya
I'll be 'kilt'
Mind the clock
Don't kick it
Go home!
There's your ticket.
Tenement clothes
Stored on shelf
Emmet and Anthony
With willow delph
One of the books
The life of Tone.
With eight-day clock
On its own
And stable
Paddy Murphy Roan.
Scholars and shawls
Move away
Surviving for another day
Will he miss
Young Emmet
At his tay.
God love us all.
Sure we have to pay.
He knows
We've got no other way.
And Emmet won't mind
Another stay
At his uncle Jemmy's.

by Eamonn Mac Thomais.

One of the many pawnbrokers who have recently closed the door,
Weafer's of Dorset Street.

The Comedy King

"I told you" my mother said, "how many more times are you going to ask me? His name is Jimmy O'Dea and he comes from a very comfortable family, his father spent pounds on his education, and he was wild when Jimmy gave up his profession to go on the stage." Later on that night my mother told me that the first time she saw him on stage he was like a little prince. She described his clothes down to the last detail. His suit, hat, shirt, and the shine on his shoes. "Oh" she said, "he was like a little prince, as if he had just stepped out of a hat box".

I was 10 years of age and had just returned home from my first visit to The Gaiety Theatre and the Jimmy O'Dea Pantomime. For many days after, my mind was filled with memories of the Gaiety, the climb up the stairs to the gallery, the wooden step-like seats, the music, the coloured lights, the white spot-light, the safety curtain which I read at least a dozen times, the smell of oranges and the funny little man named Jimmy O'Dea. That day my hands were sore from clapping so I copied the people beside me and banged my "Little Duke" boots on the gallery floor. A prince, my mother called him, well to me he was another King of Dublin — a king who made people laugh and sing, he made people happy and at times laughed himself, as the curtain kept rising and falling.

Jimmy O'Dea was a legend in his own lifetime and as I grew into my teens I seldom missed any of his shows. He was a master of comedy and left a million memories to audiences from the Provinces, Dublin and overseas. Like all the great troupers, his name was always linked with shows for the poor and deserving causes.

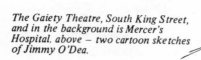
The Gaiety Theatre, South King Street, and in the background is Mercer's Hospital. above — two cartoon sketches of Jimmy O'Dea.

Harry O'Donovan, another great name in Dublin's theatreland, wrote the scripts and Jimmy brought the characters to life — together they created 'Biddy Mulligan the Pride of the Coombe', which was Jimmy's favourite role. One evening as Jimmy and Harry were walking down Henry Street, Harry said, "Jimmy, we must get you a particular type of character, something or someone that you will be recognised as; Chaplin has his Derby Hat and walking stick" ... Just at that moment a woman came out of a publichouse in Moore Street shouting at a man behind her — "Go along outa that you·bowsie". O'Donovan's eyes twinkled, his mind flashed, his fingers clicked and O'Dea soon got the message. "That's it" said Harry, "a woman of Dublin talking like that woman", and so 'Biddy' was born in the heart of Moore Street. Although Harry wrote many scripts on Moore Street, he made 'Biddy' a lady of the Liberties, who lived in the Coombe and sold her wares at Patrick Street corner.

Jimmy O'Dea was born in April, 1899 at Number Eleven Lower Bridge Street. His parents, James and Martha O'Dea were both comfortable business people. His house was three doors from where Oliver Bond lived and across the road from The Old Brazen Head Inn. Next door, Number Twelve, was Mulletts publichouse. When Jimmy was seven years of age, his aunt showed him the window in Mulletts where the true green flag of Ireland was displayed while all Dublin was decked out in Red, White and Blue.

Jimmy was born a few paces from the old Ford of Hurdles. He was baptised in St. Audoen's parish church in High Street. In his youth he served as an altar boy in the Augustinian Church, John's Lane. A good education and a good profession was planned by Jimmy's father. His first school-days were spent at The Holy Faith Prep. School at Kilcoole, Co. Wicklow. From here he went to the Marist Fathers in Dundalk, and then The Jesuits in Belvedere College, and finally to The Holy Ghost Fathers at Blackrock College.

It was agreed and decided that Jimmy would become an optician and he was apprenticed to Mr. John Murray of Number One Duke Street. Murray was a leading ophthalmic optician with branch offices at Fifty Two Queen Street, Glasgow, and One Hundred Lothian Street Edinburgh. He was also the Hon. Secretary of The Irish Optical Association. In a few years Jimmy qualified and opened his own practice in South Frederick Street Dublin. That was 1921. Six years later he left his optician's practice in the care of his sister Rita, also an optician, to become a Professional Artist.

Jimmy's early gramophone records are still in many Dublin homes, and I can remember well after my first visit to the Gaiety, volunteering every Sunday night to turn the handle of the old-style His Master's Voice type gramophone to hear Jimmy O'Dea singing about The Charladies' Ball, or Putting His Sixpence each way on Water Sprite.

THE CHARLADIES' BALL

You may talk of your outings, your picnics and parties
Your dinners and dances and hoolies and all
But wait till I tell ya the gas that we had
When we went to the Charladies' fancy-dress ball.

I was there as Queen Anne and I went with me man
He was dressed as a monkey locked up in a cage
We had pierettes and pierods and hockeytops and whatnots
And stars that you'd see on the Talkies and stage.

CHORUS

At the Charladies' Ball people said one and all
You're the belle of the ball Mrs. Mulligan
We had one-steps and two-steps and the divil knows what new ste
We swore that we'd never be done again bedad
We had wine, Guinness and Jameson
We had cocktails and cocoa and all
We had champagne all night but we'd real pains next morning
The night that we danced at the Charladies' Ball.

There were injuns and cowboys that came from Drumcondra
We had Francis Street fairies all diamonds and stars
There was one of the Rooney's like a clock over Mooney's
And a telegraph boy as a message from Mars.

Mary Moore from the Lotts was the Queen of the Scots
With a crown out'a Woolworths perched up on her dome
There was young Jimmy Whitehouse dressed up as a lighthouse
And a Camden Street Garbo that should've gone home.

CHORUS

At the Charladies' Ball people said one and all
You're the belle of the ball Mrs. Mulligan
We had one-steps and two-steps and the divil knows what new ste
We swore that we'd never be done again bedad
We had wine, porter and Jameson
We had cocktails and cocoa and all
We had rumbos and tangos, half-sets and fandangos
The night that we danced at the Charladies' Ball.

Mary Ellen O'Rourke was the Queen of the Dawn
By 1.30 she looked like a rale dirty night
Mickey Farren the betser was dressed as a jester
He burst his balloon and dropped dead with the fright.

Above:'King' Jimmy O'Dea and Maureen Potter during a skit on the Vikings which was part of the show "Home James" at the Gaiety about 1958.

Below: Harry O'Donovan in the late 1950's.

Jim Barr went as Bovril, stops that sinkin' feelin'
Astride of a bottle, pyjamas and all
He bumped into Faust who was gloriously saused
And the two of them were sunk at the end of the hall.

CHORUS

At the Charladies' Ball people said one and all
You're the belle of the ball Mrs. Mulligan
We had one-steps and two-steps and the divil knows what new steps
We swore that we'd never be done again bedad
We had wine, porter and Jameson
We had cocktails and cocoa and all
We'd a nice sit-down tea, but we fell down to supper
The night that we danced at the Charladies' Ball.

the streets of Dublin advertising 'We're still here'.

Merry Christmas

Bank of Laughter

N.G. Two-two-two-two

not worth tuppence

less **Five** *Pounds.*

you'll find the 'O'D' Show
Still Here" worth A Visit.

for the O'Dea Comp.

Jimmy O'Dea
Harry O'Donovan

e St. Dublin

Jimmy O'Dea was at home in front of the footlights and yet I heard him say, that every time the curtain went up, he got butterflies in his stomach. He loved people and was always happiest when he was in front of them on the stage, giving them his best in entertainment.

Its true to say that Dublin's great Queen of Comedy, Maureen Potter, got part of her greatness from Jimmy O'Dea. When they acted together they were the King and Queen of Dublin's comedy. She carries on the great tradition at the Gaiety today. Nevertheless, the name O'Dea must always be linked with the name O'Donovan. For close on forty years they were the leaders of Dublin's wit and comedy. When both died, part of Dublin died with them. The name and memory of O'Dea and O'Donovan will always have a special place in the hearts of all Dubliners.

The next time you go down Moore Street, listen for the real Biddy Mulligan — you might even see the twinkle in Harry O'Donovan's eyes, or the smile on Jimmy O'Dea's lips — "Its the likes of me that has the likes of you driving around in your Rolls--s Royces".

Street Characters

'Bang Bang', the famous character of the Liberties is an imposter. Yes I was shocked, I could not believe my ears, but he told me so himself, straight from Bang Bang's lips. He's a foreigner, born in the Rotunda Hospital on the north side of Dublin. And remember what my grandmother used to say — "If you have to cross Church Street Bridge to go home, you're a bloody foreigner, and you'll need a passport to re-enter the Liberties of Dublin". Well 'Bang Bang' showed me his passport — his pension book from which I jotted down the following details:-

Thomas Dudley, 50b Bridgefoot Street, Dublin.

No mention of the words Bang Bang — he told me he'd rather be called Lord Dudley. "I had no mammy or daddy" he said, "the nuns in Cabra reared me. I was born in the Rotunda. I had another mammy in Hill Street. I also lived in Newmarket — your hand is lovely and warm sir, you're a gentleman sir, ye know me, don't ye sir. I'm going blind" he said, "my eyes are very bad. I don't like where I'm living. I want to go back to the old place. Do you mind me holding your hand, sir, Lord Dudley, sir, why don't they call me Lord Dudley". "Bang Bang Lord Dudley" I said. "Its an honour to meet you again after all these years." "And me too sir, look sir, look sir, I still have it sir."

He let go my hand and from his inside coat pocket he drew his gun — a long door key worn thin and shining from constant use down the years, as he bang-banged with it all over Dublin and the Liberties. "I don't use it much now" he said, "not since I became Lord Dudley. I only use it an odd time, "BANG-BANG" he said, "YOU'RE DEAD". Whenever he was on a bus or tram they were vehicles of happiness — Bang Bang made the people laugh. He helped them to forget their worries as he played cowboys and indians with them in the streets of Dublin. Many Dublin people were seen dodging in and out of doorways and falling dead in the streets as they tried to shoot Bang Bang.

I met him in Thomas Street during the Liberties Festival, so I took him to the traditional concert of Irish Music in St. Catherine's in 1973. There I introduced Bang Bang to the audience. True to his name and tradition he took out his door key and said "Bang Bang, Bang Bang, you're dead". The audience gave him a wonderful reception and you could see their faces brighten and light up with smiles. Outside the door he said "Thank you sir, for bringing me in sir, they all know me sir, they like me too. Its a lovely church sir, its the first time I was ever in it — and they liked me sir—". "Bang Bang — Lord Dudley" I said, "not only do they like you — they love you — and whenever they write the history of the Liberties it won't be complete unless it mentions your name." He smiled, yet his eyes were sad and weak. He smiled again and half said to himself — "They like me, they like me sir". I gave him a few bob for a few jars and promised to look him up again for a chat.

He held my hand in an iron grip for twenty minutes, and again went over his life story. "You know where I live now sir, call anytime. Just ask for Lord Dudley, sir." He let go my hand, and stood at the door of Ryan's public-house, looking after me until I turned the corner at John's Lane, and was out of sight.

*   *   *

Dan Donnelly of Bull Alley became the Champion Boxer of the World when he defeated Cooper, an Englishman, in Donnelly's Hollow on the plains of the Curragh in Co. Kildare. The sugar-cane man, who lived in the spital-fields, and who sold sweet bars, told the story of the first fight over and over again. He said Donnelly was in trouble in the seventh round, and was nearly beaten, but he managed to throw a few sweet bars into Donnelly's gob, and the rest of the story is history.

Donnelly returned to Dublin leading a Victory Parade. Thousands marched while thousands of others lined the pavements cheering and singing. Donnelly was in an open carriage drawn by four white horses. His mother, a big fat woman sat beside him. When the Victory Parade reached James's Street (it took seventeen days to come from the Curragh with a stop at every public-house) his mother stripped down to the waist. Slapping her bosom now and again as she cried out, "I'm the woman who reared him, and these are the breasts that fed him". When the parade reached the Coombe, they all adjourned to the Four Corners of Hell for drinks all round. Another fight nearly started between the mother and the sugar-cane man, as they both claimed it was their product which gave Dan the strength for the Final Knockout Blow.

'The Bird' Flanagan got his name from the time he went to a fancy dress ball dressed as a bird. When he didn't win a prize, he went up onto the stage where the judge sat, laid an egg, and then threw it at the judge. 'The Bird' was a wealthy man and owned cabbage fields all over Crumlin Drimnagh, and Walkinstown. These lands at one time belonged to a man named Keogh, who was a member of the Invincibles who escaped with his family to America after Cavendish and Burke were killed in the Phoenix Park.

*   *   *

'Endymion' was a character who haunted Grafton Street and College Green. He dressed in a deerstalker hat, knee breeches, tunic shirt and buckled shoes. He always carried a few spare swords, a fishing rod and an umbrella which was always up on a fine day and down on a wet day. Sometimes he fished through the railings of Trinity College.

Endymion lived in Pleasant Street. He used a compass to find his way home from O'Connell Street daily, and he gave a sword salute to the Ballast Office clock, he would then set his alarm clock by it, wet his finger, hold it up to see which way the wind was blowing, take out his compass, get his bearing, and make for home. The compass never let him down — even when he went home via James's Street, Kilmainham, South Circular Road, Rialto Bridge, and Heytesbury Street.

*   *   *

'Zozimus', Michael Moran, the blind ballad singer, was born in Faddle Alley in 1794. He lost the sight of both eyes two weeks after birth. Its a miracle how he was able to learn so many ballads and poems and he must have had a brilliant memory. He lived all his life in the Liberties and ended his days in 14½ Patrick Street.

His friends were other street characters of the period known as 'Owny the Fool', who was as wise as an owl, 'Peg the Man', 'Fat Mary', the prima donna of the Dublin streets, 'Stoney Pockets', 'The Dear Man', and several others who performed on the streets of Dublin.

Opposite page — A rather glamourised portrait of Dan Donnelly the famous boxer, and to his right is 'Endymion' drawn in 1907 complete with sword and umbrella.

Right — the sad figure represents the famous blind ballad singer of the liberties Michael Moran, better known as 'Zozimus'

Zozimus got his name from the poem of St. Mary of Egypt written by Bishop Coyle, and the name Zozimus was mentioned many times in the poem. His only trip outside the Liberties was to Cullenswood in Ranelagh, where he entertained at the Runaway Marriages which were performed by a German clergyman named Schultz. The journeys were usually made on Bobby Tomkins' horse and dray, that is whenever the dray wasn't in the pawn office yard.

Zozimus died on the 3rd April 1846 and was buried in Glasnevin Cemetery. His grave is No.AG 30. Fr. Nicholas O'Keefe a curate of Francis Street church who later became P.P. Rush, attended him in his last illness. The day he died Zozimus said — "Excuse me your Riverence — I won't be a minute, I'm dictating me funeral arrangements". Zozimus had a great fear that the sack-em-ups would get him and he'd end up in the College of Surgeons.

A week after he died, a miniature painter named Horatio Nelson of Grafton Street produced a painting of 'Zozimus, Rhymer and Reciter'. A short time after this a man appeared in Patrick Street dressed like him, and claimed he was the real Zozimus. He went from pub to pub claiming his free whiskey droppings (the whiskey which spilled into a tray while it was being poured out). Stoney Pockets said it was a bloody good job they put Zozimus down a hole in Glasnevin because if the sack-em-ups had a got him to The College of Surgeons whiskey would have been banned for ever.

*   *   *

President Keely was another Dublin character. "The ship can't go out if it doesn't come in — the sun will never fall in Dublin it will do as I say — Vote Number One President Keely. The Ministers use only silver keys but President Keely uses gold keys". During the Presidential Elections Keely was a very busy man, and he always appeared on the day of the inauguration ceremony. He would march up Lord Edward Street pushing a handcart, wearing a tall silk hat with his name 'Keely' written on it. He always got a better ovation than the President Elect.

*   *   *

'Tie-me-Up' was another character who provided great entertainment. I never knew his real name but he always stood at the Metal Bridge, stripped to the waist, cracking a big whip and shouting "Tie me up, Tie me up". He would get a few men to tie him in chains, and then put a straight jacket on him — he'd twist, turn, roll over, twist again, his eyes would nearly burst out of his head, he'd roar with pain and then after about twelve minutes he would free himself — to the applause of the audience. The hat would then go around and for an encore he would balance a heavy cart-wheel on his chin or lie on broken glass.

*   *   *

'Spec's' was another widely known character, and again I have not uncovered his real name. He lived somewhere in Crumlin. He was over six feet tall and always had a piece of cloth tied from the front wheel to the handlebars of his bike to catch the wind, and carry him along like a sailing boat. He could peel an apple without breaking the skin and when he finished his work of art he would throw away the apple and eat the skin.

One day he asked us to put wind in his sails, so we took it he wanted the wheels of his bike pumped. This happened during the last · war when cigarettes were very scarce. When we finished the job he took a Players (blue tin) box which usually contained 100 cigarettes from his saddle bag. Our eyes nearly popped out of our heads. He said "You are very good lads and I'm going to give you three each". Spec's then opened the box and gave each of us three Conversation Lozenges — "You're Cute", "Kiss Me", "Lover Boy" etc. Well you should have heard our conversation about Spec's, his Boat-Bike and his sweets. One thing I'm sure of, it will never get into print or onto Conversation Lozenges.

*   *   *

'Lino' is another character. He got his name beçause he was always lying on the floor. At time of writing he is one of the best known and best loved characters on the northside. He is another Bang Bang type who brings happiness and joy into people's lives everyday. A lovely man, a darling man, me oul' flower Lino, more power to your elbow.

*   *   *

And we must remember Matt Talbot, loved by the poor. Dublin's Holy Man who slept on planks of wood and wore chains around his body. He died on his way to Mass in Granby Lane. Many times I heard my mother say — "Don't worry Mary. I'll get a job. Matt Talbot won't let me down". Later in the day word would come to my mother "Yes, you are to start tomorrow at 8 a.m. I think its a few months' work". "I told you Mary" my mother would

Some recently observed faces on the streets of Dublin.

say, "Matt never let me down yet, he knows what its like to be idle in Dublin and he always looks after his own." A few pennies would then go into St. Anthony's Box (bread for the poor) and my mother would say, "I'm giving it to you Anthony, but I know it was Matt the Dubliner who got me the job."

*   *   *

Siki, "Cyclone Warren" was a negro boxer who came to Dublin, fell in love with the city and its people and never left. He was a big man with big feet, and was very popular with Dubliners. At one time he was used to advertise Nugget Boot Polish. He used to stand on a piece of black wood that looked like black marble — and written on it were the words "Nugget Polish"– a very likeable character.

*   *   *

"Billy in the Bowl" (Billy Davis) was born without legs, and he used to sit in an iron bowl and with the use of his powerful arms he could push his bowl along the streets. His haunts were around Manor Street and the lanes of Oxmanstown. Billy Davis became too fond of drink and then started to rob people. He spent several short terms of imprisonment in Newgate Jail. One of the Dublin street ballads 'The Twangmans Revenge', sung by Zozimus, had the lines —

He took her out to Sandymount

To hear the waters rowl

And he won the heart of the Twangmans mot

Playing Billy in the Bowl —

Poor Billy, while robbing a man he also killed him. A witness was present, and saw Billy sliding away in his bowl. Billy was arrested, sentenced to life imprisonment and he died in jail.

*   *   *

'All Parcels' was a beggar lady who spent every day collecting waste paper. She would make it up into several neat parcels, and was a familiar sight carrying her bundles round the Liberties. Her usual haunts were Thomas Street and James's Street. Waste paper in those days, the 1930's, was valuable, and a good sack-full, of six parcels, would be worth a few pennies each day. As children, we collected waste paper for picture money, for the fourpenny rush; 'All Parcels' collected it to keep herself alive.

*   *   *

Lilian McEvoy was a Dublin street musician who used to play in O'Connell Street about 1928. The police moved her along, so she then played in Earl Street — the police moved her again and she took up another stand in Marlborough Street, outside Gogan's shop at the corner of North Earl Street. Gogan's shop was used by Michael Collins and other I.R.A. Leaders during the Black & Tan War, as a depot for dispatches.

Opposite page — Two street characters, left Davy Stephens who sold newspapers at Dun Laoghaire and 'The Professor'

Lilian later moved to Grafton Street, and one evening in 1932 she was spotted and heard by Fritz Kreisler, the world famous violinist. He was in Dublin for an engagement in the Theatre Royal. Kreisler, who had spent his life helping good street musicians all over the world, got Lilian a week's engagement in the Theatre Royal. That week, which took Lilian off the cold winter streets of Dublin, was the start of a famous stage career, and Lilian never had to play in the streets again.

She went to England and married a man named Douglas. Her daughter, Shirley Douglas, follows her mother's stage tradition, and Shirley's record 'Freight Train' is well known to skiffle group fans today. The next time you hear Shirley's records, think of her mother, the young girl from Kells, County Meath, who went to fame and fortune, from Grafton Street Dublin.

Dublin had many other characters, and here are a few of their names – Dunlavin, Hamlet, Jack the Tumbler, Uncle, Rock, Damn the Weather, Prince of Denmark, Hairy Lemon, Hairy Yank, Shell Shock Joe, The Toucher Doyle, Bugler Dunne, Jembo-no-Toes, the Blind Artillery Man, Johnny Forty Coats, Mad Mary, The Professor and Davy Stephens.

Dublin still has many characters, and I'm sure that every Dubliner has his own favourites. You know who I mean, 'yer man' in the bookies office, at the football match, on the bus, or marking his card at a game of bingo. Whenever you turn a corner in Dublin, you're sure to meet a host of characters. Of course we have some lovely jewel-and-darlin' lady characters as well, "Yer wan" in Moore Street. They have wit at their finger-tips. Talk to them and get the real feel of Dublin. Too many tourists and natives miss all this life as they move through the Streets of Dublin.

Some Dublin Slang

If Zozimus was alive today he'd have to employ an interpreter. No one would understand him and his "Newgate Cant". If he said "he was sweating his duds to ris it" his interpreter would have to explain that Zozimus was going to pawn his clothes to raise a few shillings. The old Newgate Slang had a beauty all its own, and can be found in the ballads 'Luke Caffrey's Ghost', 'De Night before Larry was Stretched', 'Mrs. Coffey', 'Larry's Ghost' and 'The Kilmainham Minuet'.

The Joly collection of song music in the National Library is well worth a close study. The Luke Caffrey in the ballad was arrested in Ram Alley beside Skinners Row opposite Christchurch Cathedral. The crowd said "If Luke hadn't of let the watch take him, that they would have skinned him alive". Luke put up a great fight, "He squar'd up to de two bailies, tip'd wan of dem a loving squeeze, den gave him a cut of bread an' butter over de elbow — the fight went on an' den he tip'd de oder a long-arm leg, mid a dig in the smellers dat laid him on his face, be de hokey — after Luke was hanged, his ghost came back looking like nutin' on earth. His eyes were swelled in his brain-box, like two scalded goose-berries in a mutton tart and his grinders rattled in his jaw-wags for all de world, like a pair of white-headed fortune-tellers in an elbow-shakers bone box — Luke wanted to tell his friends to lay off his girl-friend who was known as one-eyed Bid of de alley — and he threatened the boys that if they were at Bid he'd whitewash the walls with their brains". Luke was hanged in Kilmainham with his face towards the city.

Larry was hanged (stretched) in Newgate Jail. His wife Nell was comforted by Katto Crawley who "tipped de bottle down Nell's trottle, which opened de lights in her garret. Nell cursed de bloody old judge who gev de cramp-jaw to her Larry". She also cursed Gregg the jailer as turnkey in Newgate Jail who broke up her last visit with Larry and put all the prisoners in their cage — Gregg was the jailer who years later kicked a street-girl to death because she accused him of murdering Oliver Bond in 1798. "I see'd ye" she said, "I see'd ya, ya hit him on the scruff of de head wid a copper kittle".

Zozimus was the King of the Newgate Cant, "Have yis no other de varnishin only sticking pins in a dark man. If the watch was set or the nu po-liss out I'd make some iv ye jump Jim Crow — I feel horrible wet, am I standing in a poddel Stoney?"

Down the years, the Newgate Cant, Dublin Slang, and expressions changed with education. Yet quite a few of the old traditional ones remain. The Boss is known as *The Head Buck Cat; Fla-hool-ack* — from the Irish 'flathuil' means 'generous'. *Box the Fox* — Rob an Orchard; *The Jer* and *Mitch* —stay

away from school. *Stag* — an informer — (Major Sirrs stag house, Kilmainham). *Biffed* — slapped with a leather strap. *Stocious* — Drunk. *Jewel-an'-Darlin'* — a phrase used by Dublin women mostly to other women. *Mal-a-Voke* — *'I'll mal-a-voke ya'* — a Dublin war cry, usually a woman's. *A Wino* — cheap wine drinker. *Red Biddy* — methylated spirits and brasso. *Wizent* — denoting a small child with an older child's face — *"He's a wizent ol' man missus"*. *A Hussy* — a loose girl or a girl that wore lipstick years ago. Another insulting phrase was *"a bitch is a dog, a decent dog, but you ye pup yer nutin"*.

Laid out — a corpse dressed in a habit, prior to being coffined. *The Roto,* or *The Roxy* — The Rotunda. *The Tivo* — The Tivoli Cinema Francis Street. *Franner* — Francis Street. *The Brothers* — The Irish Christian Brothers. Here are some examples of the way some Dubliners pronounce words: *Pennert* — Pennyworth. *Joca-la* — Chocolate. *Ospidal* — Hospital. *Ceilent* — Ceiling. *Eammont* — Eamonn. *Trun it* — Threw it. *Tubacanist* — Tobacconist. *Bruid* — Bread. *None more bein gev out* — not giving out any more. *Stee-ven-ziz* — Dr. Steeven's Hospital. *Orators* — Auditors. *Dra-gool-a* — Dracula.

Up the Pole — pregnant, a term often used in reference to a single girl. *A Prayer Factory* — A convent. The modern *ben lang* — (slang) is also changing, and today's style has a certain rhyming pattern, yet some of the older words still remain. *Corn-Beef* — Chief; *Bit-an-Brace* — Face; *Mince Pies* — Eyes; *Two-by-four* — Door; *Plates of Meat* — Feet; *Fork and Knife* — Wife; *Apples and Pears* — Stairs; *Whistle and Flute* — Suit of clothes, the old type word was *clobber, duds,* and the English slang term for suit is *Tin of Fruit.* The priest is known as *The Sky Pilot. On the Ball* is begging. *The Lid* is a hat. *German Band* — Hand. *Strides* — Trousers. *Jam Jar* — Car.

One and One which means Fish and Chips comes from the days the "ities' (Italians) couldn't speak English so the Dubliners pointed 'Wan of that' and 'Wan of that' — The 'ities' caught on quickly and from a small beginning as instrument makers in the 18th century, they are all over Dublin now and nearly own O'Connell Street. There was an area in the Liberties called 'Little Italy'.

The Bay-No is a children's play centre set up by the Iveagh Trust, *Husband and Wife*, or *Out in a Box* means life imprisonment. *Peter, safe, Morning Jew, Screw* — Prison Officer. *Four by two* — a Jew. *One by two* — a shoe. *A Kevin Barry* — A Brave Person. *A Jemmy* — A tool. *A Long Distance Man* is one who stops in the best hotels for one night and leaves next morning with the best silver. *Working the Oracle* — pulling rabbits out of a hat or *pulling a quick one* all mean roughly the same thing.

A wagon, a nut, a head case, a lu-la, a fruit-'n'-nut, stir crazy, all mean a mad man, but each phrase has a subtlety all its own. *A Paraffin Lamp* means a Tramp. *Chicken's Neck* is a cheque — a dud one. *Croak* — Dead. *The Naller* — The Canal. *The Flicks* — The Pictures (Cinema). *A Claud* or *A Wing* — A Penny. *A Make* — A Halfpenny. *"He's not the full shilling", "He's touched", "He's not all there"* means he's crazy. *Mouth Organs* — Pigs' Feet. *Stubbed* — No response at door. *Rat* — A mean person.

Under the hammer was a term used in coal yards when workers did not earn the full minimum wage. *Drum and Gaff* — Housebreaking. *Richard the Third* or *Bird* — a girl. *Collecting Flake* — Picking up cigarette butts from the gutter. *A Pavement Hostess* — A Street Girl. *Guino* — Money. *The Holy Hour* refers to the hour (2.30 — 3.30) when publichouses close their doors to get the people home for their dinners. This closing hour was passed by law. *Skidaddle* — move along.

Back again to the rhyme slang. Here is a sample — *A battle cruiser* — *Boozer* — Publichouse. *Peggy Dell* — Cell. *Teddy Bear* — Hair. *Uncle Ned* — Head. *Donald Pears* — Ears. *Bars in the Grate* — Teeth. *North and South* — Mouth. *Rambling Rose* — Nose. *Scotch-Peg* — Leg. *Bees and Honey* — Money. *Needle and Thread* — Bed. *Bottle and Stoppers* — Police (Coppers). *Joe Skinner* — Dinner. *Belinda Lee* — Tea. *King Farouks* — Books. *Linen Drapers* — Papers. *A Bull and Cow* — Row. *Daisy Roots* — Boots. *Tom Dick* — Sick. *Nelson Eddies* and *Reddies* — Money. *The Goggle Box* — T.V. *Town Hall* — Football. *Skin and Blister* — Sister. *One and Other* — Brother. *Cain and Abel* — Table. *Tit for Tat* — Chat. *Laughing Jokes* — Smokes, Cigarettes (Fags). *Ships Hatchet* — Matches. *Kitchen Range* — Change. *Sky Rocket* — Pocket. *Roast Joint* — Pint. *Mother and Daughter* — Water.

A mixture of Irish and English and old-time slang is used widely today and a *gansey load* in the 1930's still means a gansey load to the childer of 1974 — A gansey load means your jersey full of apples after a night at the ol' *Box the Fox.*

"Do you know what I'm going to tell ya Mister T, like ya know like, I'm gone off me food. I'm not the same man at all at all, no its me liver like, giving me hell. As the Misses says 'Doctors differ and patients die'. Well, Mr. T they can differ all they *bloodywellike* but none of them is doing the damn thing any good, me liver I mean". The man with the bad liver spreads six cream buns on the wooden seat of the workers' hut, then he opens a tin of sardines and he sticks a few sardines into each cream bun and sprinkles each bun with a drop of fish oil, fills his jam-jar with tea and eats and drinks the lot in four minutes flat. Then he says "Naw –didn't enjoy it, I'm really gone off me food, the liver is a terrible thing, its worser than the heart. Why does it have to be me Mister T, like ya know like I'm no bowsie, gurrier or gowger. I take care of me health like. I'm very fussy about what I eat and drink." Another Dubliner comes on the scene and he says to the man with the bad liver "I don't want to worry ya like Pat. Far be it from me to worry ya, but that bloody liver's goin' to kill ya like, and I know be the *lookofya* that yer gone off yer food — ah well as long as ya keep the roof over yer head that's all that matthers. Amn't I right Mister T. Keep the roof over yer head and *yalbe* as happy as Larry."

I often wondered who was Larry, and why he was always happy. Was it Larry the Lockman at the second lock on the Grand Canal, Goldenbridge? or was it Larry Burn of Glenmalure House Rialto, who had the only. public-house in Dublin where the grass grew under your feet as you stood at the bar. However, just before the lawn had fully grown between the floor-boards Larry sold out and a modern pub marks the historic site today. "Happy as Larry" well we can be sure it wasn't Larry the night before he was stretched.

But then everyone wasn't always happy. "See yer man, he has a face that would stop a clock" or "Yer man — he has a face like a plateful of mortal sins". I don't think anyone in the world can tell what a mortaller (mortal sin) looks like — but the Dubliner, ah well they're different like — they can tell ya what a 'plateful of mortal sins' looks like!

Sound Smell and Colour

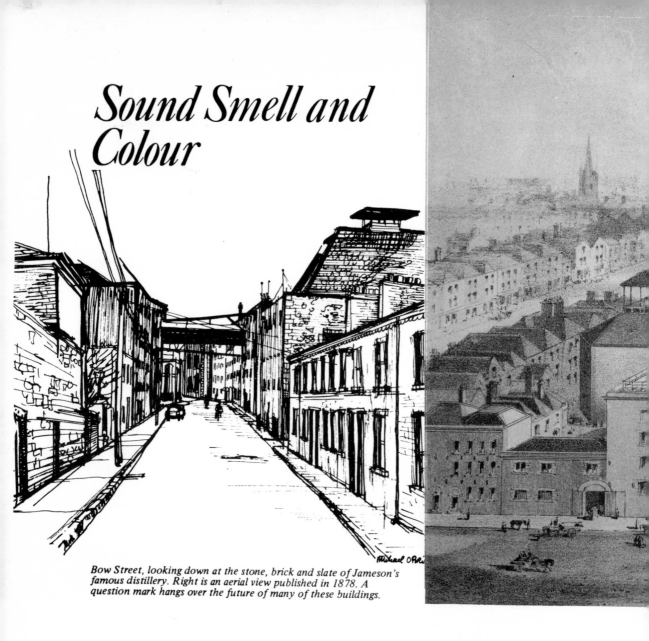

Bow Street, looking down at the stone, brick and slate of Jameson's famous distillery. Right is an aerial view published in 1878. A question mark hangs over the future of many of these buildings.

Listen to Dublin. Listen to its heart beating, its children laughing or crying. Listen for the Dalymount roar or the cultured cry from Hill Sixteen in Croke Park. Listen to the dealers in the streets, and the jingle sounds of silver and copper coins in their apron pockets. Listen for the footsteps or the odd horse-car go over grey cobblestones, or seagulls screeching over waste-bins at Mountjoy prison or around the fishing boats at Howth Harbour.

The sounds of churchbells ringing, clocks striking, rivers and canals flowing and the sound of a train, the foghorn and the factory hooter. Listen for the sound of Dublin wit wherever Dubliners are gathered. The Firebrigade and Ambulance services lead the way in Dublin siren sounds. The steel demolition ball crushing to dust our historic houses and electric hammers dancing on our streets and roads. The sound of silence in the hollow of the Phoenix Park

after the band and the people have gone home, and the strange foreign sounds from the cages and pits in Dublin Zoo.

The sounds of Dublin are changing daily. Gone forever are the old familiar magical sounds of 'Coal Blocks, Coal Blocks, what do you feed your mother on?' 'Coal Blocks, Hearilly Mail, Hearilly Mail, Stop Press, Read all about it, Stop Press, Sweet Lavender, Water Cress, Taffey Apples, Taffey Apples, get your windy mills, rags, bottles, jam-jars, and bones, windy mills and bones'. The ringing of the coal man's bell tied to the horse's head has been replaced by central heating which brings us to the smells of Dublin, when the boiler breaks down or goes haywire.

'Go down to Moore Street', said the late Jimmy O'Dea, the Dublin comedian, 'and get your nose educated'. Nose education in Dublin is second to none in the world. To qualify for a diploma you must be able to stand on Ward Hill in the Liberties and see if your nose can cope with the smell from O'Keefe's the Knackers' yard, and tell the difference between the smells from the Liffey's forty shades of green, each with its own peculiar smell.

Ah but there are other smells in Dublin, as sweet as honey, or as fragrant as newmown hay — the smell of the fish-and-chipper on a cold winter's night, sometimes they even smell better than they taste. The smell of Jacob's Biscuits in Bishop Street, Willwood Jams in Parnell Street, and Mackintosh's Chocolate in Kilmainham — the deep smell of hops and porter at James's Gate. Until recently if you preferred the other stuff, the hard tack, you went over to Hangman's Lane and walked slowly towards Smithfield and the Red Cow — you could nearly smell yourself drunk. The smell of pig yards in the gardens of Georgian mansions, or Cooper's horse stables in Queen Street, which will remind you of the Horse Show in Ballsbridge.

Off Capel Street you will find the Fruit and Vegetable Market. The drawing shows the main entrance crowned with the arms of Dublin. It was erected in 1892. Nearby is the Fish Market and also The Daisy Market.

*Can you imagine the smell and noise of cattle being driven down Red Cow Lane towards Smithfield?
The chimney at the end is part of Jameson's Distillery.*

Inhale for your life's worth the odour of the fish and fruit markets, or children at the pictures (cinema) eating crisps, popcorn and oranges. You can still wallow in the smell of Lemon's Sweets on the banks of the Tolka, and it doesn't have to be a Saturday either. Strawberry, raspberry, pineapple, greengage, you name the flavour, and there you can smell it.

Enjoy the aroma from Bewley's shops when the coffee is being ground, or brewed, or just displayed in the windows like small brown mountains. At Hallowe'en you can smell Bewley's barm bracks all over Dublin. The man on the bus with a sup too much or the new-born babe in its mother's arms, incense and candles burning while people pray together at the countless shrines — they all make up the smells of Dublin, the nice ones and the bitter ones.

The pork butchers with their meats, sausages, peppers and seasonings, the fresh bread from the bakery, a rasher-and-egg frying on a shovel over a coke fire in a watchman's hut are enough to make your tongue water. What are your favourite smells of Dublin? or do you leave all that sort of thing to the Bisto Kids?

What colour is Dublin City? Gold, silver, and battleship grey, or rich warm red and brown, blue skies speckled with large and small green domes and grey spires? Transparent windows in a million office blocks with bronze and brass-coloured name plates and letter boxes.

The multicoloured wall of a Capel Street shop and the black-and-white pillars of the old Parliament House, at present being lovingly cleaned. The ever-

What would Grafton Street be without the beautiful smell of Bewley's coffee?

changing colours of Dame Street. Trinity College is like a framed picture with its white window frames surrounded by the rich greys of expert stonework. The green leaf trees along the banks of the Liffey are reflected in the changing colours of her waters. Observe the golden letters and harp on the Parnell Monument and the statue of Mr. Gray watching the colourful scene at Abbey Street corner.

The Black Diamond Mountains in Dublin Port provide heat for half the city. The red-and-grey gasometers contrast with the blue-and-yellow buoys near the Baily Lighthouse and the grey-and-white majestic Custom House which is Dublin's glory on a sunny day.

At night the neon lights provide movement and colour. The first illuminated sign I remember seeing in Dublin was the Bovril sign high over College Green. What a spectacle it provided as it burst into a rainbow of colours. The silver-studded wood on the Ha'penny Bridge dates from 1816 and its not far from the spot where Hector Grey stands on a Sunday, selling his wares.

Undoubtedly the most colourful thing about Dublin is its people. Men, women and children who are colourful in speech and manner, and only waiting to give a smile and have a chat with a friend, or a visitor.

The strange archway leads to Cooper's the horse dealers of Queen Street.

Dublin's Old Newspapers

If you ever get bored, fed up, or as a Dubliner would say, 'browned-off' go down to The National Library in Kildare Street, climb the stone staircase, push in the door and ask "yer man" behind the counter to let you have a look at *The Dublin Penny Journal, The Freeman's Journal,* the old *Irish Times Weekly, Dublin Evening Post* or *The Dublin Chronicle.* Ask for *The Correspondent,* a paper which firmly supported the establishment — it was printed in the early 1800's, firstly by E. Dowling of 1a College Green — and later by J. Martin at 11 Fleet Street. *The Comet,* a Sunday paper which first appeared on May 1st 1831 and one of its aims was to keep an uncompromising eye "upon ecclesiastical hypocrisy, cant and humbug". It was printed by Brown & Sheehan at 10 D'Olier Street. Ask also for young Paddy Kelly's *Budget.* The magic of the papers will soon have you in wonderland — I'll bet the next time you go you will bring a great big notebook and a few biros. Now if you are feeling depressed and want to get your spirit and your blood up, well then ask for *The Nation, The Irish Felon,* or the *Eye Opener.* The Editor of *Eye Opener* was a man named McIntyre. He was by no means a Republican and his paper contained a good few anti-Irish articles. Nevertheless, he was arrested in 1916 and taken prisoner to Portobello Barracks, where he was murdered along with Sheehy-Skeffington and another man named Kelly. None of the three men were in any way connected with the 1916 Rising.

Also ask for *Zozimus* and *The Irish People,* the Fenian newspaper, or John Mitchell's *United Irishman* (1848), the *Wolfe Tone Weekly* or *An Phoblacht.* Someone said one time that Dubliners speak and spend words like sailors. Well, you can take my word for it, they wrote them for the sailors of the world — and newspapers were not ten a penny either; in fact they were a bit on the expensive side. *The Nation* newspaper was sixpence in 1842; other papers were fourpence each or eight camacks — or you could say four clauds, or four wings, or eight makes — all of which added up to four old pence.

The written word was always in demand in Dublin. The first newspapers appeared in the 16th century and were a small type of almanack, which told you the type of dinner you were going to have in three weeks' time. Star-gazing was a popular art and all the future visions were recorded in words. In the early 17th century *Pue's Occurrences* appeared and was accepted as the official organ of Dublin. Next on the scene was *Dublin Intelligence.* The first Republican revolutionary newspaper to reach the streets of Dublin was the Belfast-printed and published *Northern Star,* official organ of the United Irishmen. This was edited by Samuel Neilson and distributed by Dr. Brennan in Dame Street under the eyes of Dublin Castle.

May.

GEORGE FAULKNER. NUMB. 3868
The Dublin Journal.

From SATURDAY May the 19th, to TUESDAY May the 22d, 1764.

The Volunteers Journal; Or, IRISH HERALD.

Printed and published at No. 7, DAME-STREET, Corner of PALACE-STREET. [LETTER-BOX in Palace-Street.]

Price Two-Pence.] WEDNESDAY, AUGUST 16, 1786. [No. 357

VOL. IX.   No. 93.

THE
MORNING POST, OR,
DUBLIN COURANT.

PRICE TWO-PENCE. THURSDAY, AUGUST 11, 1796.

A REVIEW OF THE SEVENTH SESSION OF THE FIFTH

POSITIVELY
MADAM MARA's LAST PERFORMANCE IN THIS CITY.
MR. FLORIO's BENEFIT.

HAMILTON LILLY,
BEGS leave to acquaint his Friends and Customers, that he has removed from

SAUNDERS'S NEWS-LETTER, and Daily Advertiser.

No. 2896   THURSDAY, AUGUST 23, 1798   Price Three-pence

FOREIGN INTELLIGENCE

THE CONSTITUTION;
OR,
Anti-Union Evening Post.

THURSDAY, MAY 29, 1800.

The Nation newspaper, founded by the Young Irelanders — Davis, Duffy and Dillon moved a little further away and had their offices in Abbey Street where *The Independent* Newspapers' offices stand today. John Mitchel wasn't too fussy about The Castle; his office was in Trinity Street, but his paper *The United Irishman* only lasted for six issues before it was suppressed and Mitchel was sent in chains to Van Diemen's Land. *The Irish Felon,* edited by Thomas Delvin Reilly and John Martin was also printed in Trinity Street and it too was suppressed and its editors jailed.

"Damn the Castle" said Thomas Clarke Luby, Editor of *The Irish People,* organ of The Fenian Brotherhood, as he sat at his Editor's desk in their offices at 12 Parliament Street. O'Donovan Rossa was the Business Manager, but it wasn't long until the Castle troops raided and suppressed the paper and sent Clarke, Luby and Rossa to penal servitude for twenty years in British dungeons. *Zozimus* (1870) started by A.M. Sullivan from the *Nation* office in Abbey Street got its name and cover from Michael Moran, the blind ballad singer. The cover showed Zozimus chasing English comics out of Ireland. Pimlico, Charlemont Street and Liberty Hall were the places where Connolly edited and wrote his *Workers Republic,* the organ of The Irish Citizen Army. *The Irish Volunteer* which gave details of history and the trade of arms for war was published at 65 Middle Abbey Street Dublin. In the 1913-1914 issues are some very interesting articles on The Irish Volunteers of 1782, and an article by The O'Rahilly on the Flag Colours for every county in Ireland. This article was written as a suggestion to each Volunteer Company to enable them to design their own Brigade Flags.

From the Dublin Central Wolfe Tone Club Committee (I.R.B.) came the idea for *The Irish Freedom* newspaper — Tom Clarke, Sean MacDiarmada (both executed 1916) were the guiding lights — Tom acted as Chairman and Sean as Treasurer on the Editorial Committee. The first issue was on sale on 1st November 1910. The Editorial Address was given at 7 Sinnot Place, off Dorset Street. Later the offices were moved to 5 Findlater's Place and in May 1914 the office was again moved, this time to 12 D'Olier Street. Among the contributors were Patrick Pearse and Terence McSwiney. McSwiney died on hunger strike in Brixton Prison in October 1920, after a 75-day fast. Pat McCartan was Editor. Most of the work and contacts made were at Tom Clarke's shop at 75A Parnell Street. An old photograph shows the small shop with Tom at the Door —

T. S. O'Cleirig / Tom Clarke, Tobacconist & Stationer

The shop window had the number 75A in the centre and also stated "Branch at 55 Amiens Street". Newspaper posters outside the shop read as follows:-

First on top   *Irish Freedom*
and next   *The Principles of Freedom*

which was Terence McSwiney's book, then available in pamphlet form. Next came an advertisement for *Tit-Bits, Ireland's Own, Boxing World, Daily Sketch*

The Patriot

WEDNESDAY, DECEMBER 7, 1814.   [NUMBER 1315]

The ✻ Star,
AND FASHIONABLE WORLD.

NUMBER 217.]   DUBLIN, MONDAY, OCTOBER 11, 1824.   [PRICE FIVE-PENCE.

The Irish Independent
TRADE AND LABOUR JOURNAL.

For the cause that lacks assistance,
For the wrongs that need resistance,
For the future in the distance,
For all the good that we can do.—GUTHRIE.

VOL. I.—No. 5.   DUBLIN, SATURDAY, OCTOBER 11, 1873.   PRICE—ONE PENNY.
(STAMPED, THREE HALFPENCE.

NATIONAL PROSPERITY
AND
UNIVERSAL EMANCIPATION.

CAPITAL AND LABOUR.

It may be singular, and it is certainly not un-
...that the extra Parliamentary

...nation liable to be weakened or distracted
by internal dissensions, for there is but one
object involved, and that object is the protection of labour against the misapplication
of capital. Union, and singleness of purpose,
and well-directed effort, applied in a legiti-
mate and just cause, have already done much

of the promoters of the agitation for the rights
of the agricultural classes of Ireland. No one
can say that he has not judgment enough to
form an accurate estimate of the probable
action of the labour movement with reference
to other public questions, and no one we think
will venture to assert that if he had come to

sight and smell, and to the moral instincts.
Political economists tell us this terrible in-
equality is the inseparable result of a high de-
gree of civilisation. If so, the sooner we go
back into our primitive barbarism the better.
We are not political economists, nor is political
economy our theme

The Irishman.
(Registered for Transmission Abroad)

VOL. XVIII.—NO 12   DUBLIN SATURDAY, SEPTEMBER 25, 1875.   SINGLE PAPER { UNSTAMPED, 2d.
BY POST 2½d

THE ★IRISH★VOLUNTEER★
❈ ❈ AN C-ÓZLÁC ❈ ❈

Vol. 1. No. 19.   Saturday, June 13, 1914   Price, 1d.

others...ee that we want it so badly that
...are quite...ditions in the attempt to
...in it. Some, too, say that the Irish Volunteer...will help the Ulster Volunteers

served by raising any element of distrust
between members of an organisation whose
great outstanding characteristic should be
a spirit of mutual trust and comradeship.

Why The Proclamation.

In almost every county in Ireland public bodies have demanded the withdrawal
of the proclamation, forbidding the im-

— on the far side posters for *The Diamond, Racing Judge* and *The Irish Times* — which gives some idea of the reading matter that was available at the period.

A hundred years ago there were more comics and papers written and printed in Dublin than in London. The old Thoms' Directory of 1917 lists 127 Dublin printed and published papers and pamphlets which cover every aspect of life and religion. Even a brief study of old copies would be rewarding of *The Irish Builder, Shamrock and Emerald, Irish Citizen* and the *Catholic Bulletin* (Gills) which was the first to record in detail the full account of the 1916 Easter Week Rising. The other masterpiece on 1916 is the *Irish Times' Sinn Fein Rebellion Handbook* which contains a full report of the British Commission set up after the Rising. Many of the books on the 1916 Rising were written from these two sources.

[37]

The Irish Times is Dublin's and Ireland's oldest daily newspaper and its slogan is "If you miss The Irish Times you miss part of the day". It is also good to see that we still have Ireland's Own with us, it's published in Wexford and loaded with information and light reading, which includes the Pen Pals' Corner, and their slogan is "The week wouldn't be the same without Ireland's Own". Our Boys is another paper which dates back to the pre-1916 period and is mainly sold in schools.

Another source of great amusement and information are the advertisements. It is nice to come across an old advertisement for a business still in existence, and how strange and quaint they sound today. Its also a surprise to see announcements of hundreds and hundreds of firms long since gone, and the strange trades, products and activities long since forgotten.

Faulkners Journal was a dullish newspaper which could always be relied upon to support the establishment. It had a long history stretching back to the middle of the 18th century and continued till 1825 when it was bought up by The Irish Times. Faulkners had an extensive publishing business and they printed and published many interesting books. Their offices and works were at 27 Parliament Street. This street provided a home for many newspapers and printers over the years. In addition to The Irish People already mentioned, The Daily Express in 1917 had offices at 39 and 40, and at the corner, a few doors up were the offices and works of the daily Evening Mail." Herrelly Mail... Paper Sir, Paper Sir. Herrelly Mail." Dublin lost something when the old Evening Mail closed down. At one time they brought out a weekly paper as well. The Evening Mail was always regarded as a Protestant paper, yet if you were looking for a job, it was always the long columns of 'Situations Vacant' in the Mail everyone turned to. If you felt sore about anything, it was to the Evening Mail you sent your letter – "Write to the Mail about it" became as familiar as senna pods – or the Bovril sign in College Green. I even remember one time winning £5 on the Evening Mail Leading Article (Editorial). Coupons were a shilling each, the same as football or horse-racing.

The first thing we looked at in the Mail was the title of the Leading Article, then we read Mandrake the Magician (cartoon) and over to the Letters Page. Whether you agreed or not the Mail always spoke out in the honest Huguenot tradition of its famous owner-editor Joseph Sheridan Le Fanu, who took over the paper in 1842. He was born at 45 Dominick Street on 28th August 1814. He studied law at Trinity College but as soon as he graduated, he changed the wig and gown for the quill and ink. He wrote several books and can be truly acclaimed as Dublin's Edgar Alan Poe for his brilliant ghost stories.

He also bought The Dublin University Magazine and it was in this magazine that his serial story The House by the Churchyard first appeared under the pen name Charles de Cresseron. The setting was the house and churchyard in Chapelizod where he spent his childhood days. He died in 70 Merrion Square in 1873.

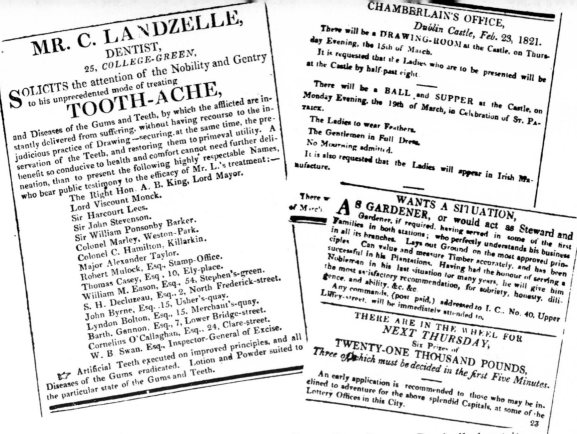
Gone forever is the old "Stop Press, Stop Press — Read all about it — Stop Press — Herrelly Mail, Herrelly Mail, Paper Sir — Paper — Sorry I can't read — Well ya can look at the bloody pictures can't ya?"

Many papers and comics went out of existence because they took a strong political stand. The one that had no worries in this direction was *The Dublin Gazette,* which was printed and published every Tuesday and Thursday from Number 8 and 9 Crow Street by the King's authority! This paper was started by King James II in 1689 but after he disappeared from the scene the paper ceased to appear. Sixteen years later another *Dublin Gazette* appeared "Published by Authority" at The Custom House Printing Office at Crane Lane off Dame Street.

Fish and chips wrapped in a sheet of newspaper provides eating, reading and education, and you need no fancy firelighters when you have a paper handy. I've seen them used for many purposes — tablecloths, and blankets on tramps in the Phoenix Park, across the chest or under the coat to keep out the wind and rain— or making small cone-shaped bags for sweets or monkey nuts. I've made them into dolls for little girls and aeroplanes or Napoleon hats for little boys.

Dublin has a great tradition in the written word. Its a far cry from quill and ink to the modern printing and colour presses of today. The Dublin writers of old claimed they were the true successors of The Bards of Di — Goddess of the Moon, and many used the pen name 'Lady Di'. My favourite Lady Di today is Nell McCafferty of *The Irish Times.*

Old Dublin Town

Dublins Many Liberties

THOMAS COURT AND DONORE

Thomas Street Dublin gets its name from Thomas-a-Becket the martyred Archbishop of Canterbury. It was the murder of Becket which gave Dublin its first liberty. King Henry II came to Ireland in the year 1171. His army marched to Dublin where he spent the Christmas season. One day he rode out to St. Catherine's Church and picked a site of land beside it. "Here", he said, "let an abbey be founded and dedicated to our holy martyr Thomas-a-Becket". He then gave the lease of lands to the Victorine Canons to build their abbey. He also gave them a special liberty owing allegiance to no one but God and the King.

Six years later Laurence O'Toole laid the foundation-stone and the first Abbot was William Fitz-Adlem. The Abbey soon spread out to take in the lands of Donore and so became known as The Liberty of Thomas Court and Donore. This royal foundation received royal grants and other charters giving it more lands and property throughout the country. The Abbey had its own palace, church, courts, gallows, prisons, graveyard and orchard gardens. Later it diverted the city water supply and had its own watercourse and mills.

It gathered taxes and also had fishing rights on the River Liffey. The Abbey became the wealthiest and most powerful in Ireland. Strongbow's sister Basila ended her days in the Abbey's guesthouse. Myles de Cogan and Hugh de

Grey Square off Grey Street.

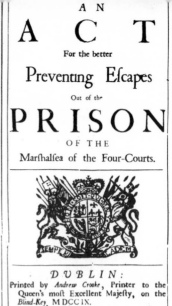

A N
A C T
For the better
Preventing Escapes
Out of the
PRISON
OF THE
Marfhalfea of the Four-Courts.

D U B L I N :
Printed by *Andrew Crooke*, Printer to the
Queen's moft Excellent Majefty, on the
Blind-Key, M DCC IX.

An old drawing of the Quadrangle of the Four Courts Marshalsea Prison. It was completely demolished early in 1974.
Right the title page of an Act of Queen Anne.

Lacy both gave large grants of land and gold to the Abbey. King John later confirmed Henry's Liberty and issued a charter to this effect.

Hugh de Lacy was killed in action in Durrow. His last Will stated that
all his wealth and property were to be given to the Abbey and that his body
was to be buried in its vaults. However, the monks of Bective Abbey, County
Meath, took de Lacy's body from Durrow and buried it in their own churchyard. The Abbot of Thomas Court and Donore was furious and demanded that
the body be brought to Dublin. The monks in Bective refused to hand over the
body. A great row developed and in order to try and solve the problem the
monks in Bective cut off de Lacy's head and sent it to Dublin. This only made
matters worse. The Abbot of St. Thomas' went to the courts, a commission
was set up and after several years the rest of the body was sent to Dublin. The
Bective churchyard can still be seen today, while there is no trace whatsoever
of the graves or vaults of St. Thomas' Abbey.

EARL OF MEATH'S LIBERTY

On 31st March 1539 the Abbey, its lands, property, malt mills and
double mills were handed over lock, stock and barrel to William Brabazon
forever. An annual rent of 18s. 6d. was levied on the lands and property —
William Brabazon was the King's Chancellor and Treasurer in Ireland — The
Abbey church was suppressed on 30th October, 1540. The Brabazons later
became the Barons of Ardee, and later still became the Earls of Meath and this
is how the area got its name, The Earl of Meath's Liberty.

The Liberty lands in Dublin took in Dolphin's Barn, Harold's Cross,
James's Street, Pimlico, Marrowbone Lane, Meath Street, Bridgefoot Street,
Thomas Street, and all the lanes and alleys in the neighbourhood. Within these
confines are numerous dwellings steeped in history. The infamous Debtors'

Prison beside Emmet's Depot in Marshalsea Lane, and nearby 151-153 Thomas Street, where Lord Edward Fitzgerald was arrested. The owner of this house, Nicholas Murphy was also arrested and became penniless as a result of his loyalty to Lord Edward.

At St. Catherine's in Thomas Street Robert Emmet was hanged and beheaded on 20th September 1803 — the funerals of the Young Irelanders and the Fenian chiefs and brave Tom Ashe stopped here also for a moment on their way to Glasnevin Cemetery. James Connolly once lived in Pimlico, an area that was once part of the Abbey grounds.

The White Bull Inn was one of the many old drinking houses with interesting names, long since vanished. Here in Thomas Street the rebels of 1798 and 1803 met and it was a few doors from Nicholas Murphy's house. The Black Bull Inn was just at the corner of Bridgefoot Street nearby. It was in the Black Bull in 1766 that two pirates were captured and later hanged on Misery Hill. Their names were McKinlie and Gidley. Together with a man named Zekerman and another named St. Quintin they took over the *Sandwick* at sea, and robbed her cargo of gold ingots and dust, jewels and Spanish milled dollars. They were traced from Wexford where they landed and were arrested in New Ross, and also the Black Bull Inn.

The Yellow Bottle Inn near where Thomas Street Library stands today was another favourite meeting-place of the United Irishmen. If you go up that way on a Saturday night you will hear beautiful Irish music coming from the Pipers Club. For this surely is Potts, Rowesome and Seery country – where fine musicians gather, and play their Irish traditional airs in the ancient lands of Dublin's first liberty.

Looking down Vicar Street towards Thomas Street. The elaborate spire belongs to John's Lane Church. It became known as the Fenian Church because of the number of Fenians who helped to build it. See page 56.

AILRED'S LIBERTY

The Second Liberty of Dublin came from Rome. In the year 1188 Ailred the Dane and his wife returned to their home which was just outside the Newgate Wall in Dublin. They had been on a pilgrimage to the Holy Land and when they entered Dublin by St. Audoen's Arch they both carried sprays of palm. From that day onwards he was known as Ailred the Palmer. He also owned lands in Rathmines and Chapelizod, and this is how we get the names of Palmerstown and Palmerston.

Ailred and his wife were very rich and were many years married but however were childless. Three days after they returned home Ailred told his wife that he was going to become a priest — "Oh you are, are ye", the wife said, "well bedad if you do I'll become a nun". "Its agreed" he said. "What order or rule will we adopt" — "The rule of St. Augustine" she said. "We will open a hospital" said Ailred "a hospital of St. John like the one in the Holy City".

In the year 1151, John Hircan, Prince of the Jews ordered that a leper hospital be built at the Tower of Tancred near St. Eithne's Gate in Jerusalem. This was the first hospital in the world. Ailred and his wife founded the second in Thomas Street, where John's Lane Church stands today. Ailred the prior and his monks nursed and cared for the sick, while the nuns made the vestments for the Canons of Dublin and also cooked the food and cleaned the hospital.

Ailred received his Liberty from Pope Clement III. This put the hospital and priory completely under Rome and exempt from the city jurisdiction. Ailred's Liberty took in his own lands of Thomas Street and part of Francis Street and Vicar Street. On the other side, the lands were bordered by the Liffey and city walls. The hospital continued to thrive until the year 1540. Kelly's timber yard opposite John's Lane Church was the priory graveyard, where the remains of Ailred, his wife and the other Holy followers of St. Augustine lie today.

An ancient site in Thomas Street, the unusual
entrance to Kelly's Timber Yard.

The present Church of St. Nicholas of Myra in Francis Street. Centre – The spire of St. Patrick's Cathedral looks down o.

The Augustines were on the run for 240 years and have a magnificent history which would fill many books. Their church today called by John Ruskin 'A Poem in Stone' was built by Fenian stonemasons and labourers. The clerk of works on the job was none other than the Pagan O'Leary, the great Fenian, who said "we were better men when we were pagans, pity St. Patrick ever found us". The impressive entrance is in Thomas Street .

A few doors away from Kelly's Timber Yard stood the publichouse where James Connolly founded his Socialist Party. Vicar Street Guardhouse can still be seen today where the bodies of Lord Kilwarden and his nephew were brought after their carriage was attacked in the Emmet Rising. Vicar Street also held the city labour yard where poor men and women had to do a hard day's work for a bowl of soup and a hunk of bread.

In John's Lane beside the church Anne Devlin lived in a garret before moving to Little Elbow Lane in the Coombe. Behind the church stands Mullinahack, a corruption of *Muilleann Salad (dirty mill)* from the waters coming down Dirty Lane (Bridgefoot Street). This is another place in Dublin where you can feel and sense the past.

On a plot of ground (Francis Street) owned by Ralph le Porter, an order of Franciscans, or Grey Friars, was founded in the year 1235. Near this church stood the church of St. Nicholas of Myra, with Carmelites, which was the poorest of religious houses in Dublin. In the year 1534 Silken Thomas used the grounds of this to brief his men for the attack on Dublin Castle. Parts of this Liberty were divided among William Brabazon, Thomas Stephens, William

...lace of St. Sepulchre's, now used as a garda station.   Right – the beautiful stone carved piers of the Palace are still in place.

Hande, Thomas Luttrell and J. Seagrave. Stephens later sold all the church property to merchants from England.

SAINT SEPULCHRE'S

Laurence O'Toole is dead. A new Archbishop of Dublin has arrived from England. His name is John Comyn and he is the first Anglo-Norman to rule the See. His residence stands beside the priory of the Holy Trinity (Christchurch) and within the civic jurisdiction. A few years later he takes a walk down to the site of St. Patrick's Well. After his visit and his prayers he looks around and finds a suitable site to build his palace, well outside the city wall. The Palace of Colonia was soon erected. It transpired that Comyn was given these lands by King John, though by right they belonged to Christchurch Cathedral.

Comyn now turned his attention to the small church at St. Patrick's Well and decided that on this site he would build a new church to God, Our Blessed Lady Mary and St. Patrick. This church was solemnly dedicated on St. Patrick's Day, 17th March 1191. Comyn now tried to abolish the cathedral of Christchurch, and operate from St. Patrick's where he had his own Liberty of Colonia. He failed and that is why we have two cathedrals today. He did gain a charter from the King for his Liberty and later changed the name of his palace and Liberty to that of St. (Holy) Sepulchre.   Heraclius, the Patriarch of Jerusalem wrote to Comyn to pray for an increase of interest in the crusades for the recovery of the Holy Sepulchre from infidel hands. The Liberty became known as the Archbishop's Liberty of St. Sepulchre.

St. Patrick's Close. Left is the Cathedral and in the background is Marsh's Library, both open to the public. Next is the Garda Station and in the right foreground is the Cathedral Grammar School.

The Archbishop's palace is now Kevin Street Garda Station with only the gate-posts, a coat of arms and a window as relics of its historic past. The Liberty of St. Sepulchre ran as far as Tallaght and Milltown and included The Coombe and Cork Street, and stretched out to South Circular Road, into Harold's Cross. Here it was divided from the Liberty of Thomas Court and Donore by the waters of the River Poddle. The Archbishop had his own courts, prisons and gallows, and was indeed a very powerful man.

DEAN'S LIBERTY

At a later stage a Liberty was granted to the Dean and chapter of St. Patrick's and this was known as the Dean's Liberty. He too had his own courts and owned the lands by St. Patrick's Park, Bull Alley and Golden Lane. Down the years there have been many disagreements between the Archbishop and the Dean over Liberties and Courts.

Sandwiched between the palace of St. Sepulchre (the garda station) and St. Patrick's is the oldest public library in Ireland. It was founded by Archbishop Marsh and built in 1701. The beautiful dark oak interior has remained unchanged for nearly three hundred years. Here you will find enough material for a lifetime's study — 25,000 books relating to the 16th, 17th and early part of the 18th centuries. The oldest book in the library is Cicero's 'Letters to his Friends', printed in Milan in 1472, and there are some older manuscripts too.

Across the road from St. Patrick's Cathedral was Emmet's Depot, 26 Patrick Street and next-door was P. J. McCall's publichouse. P. J. was a poet and scribe of the Liberties who loved and knew this area like the back of his hand. When is someone going to erect a monument to him in Patrick's Park? It was around this area that Clarence Mangan wrote his poetry and Dan Donnelly learned boxing. John Field the composer played here as a child, and

John Austin, the Jesuit who founded Saul Court Academy went to Dean Swift's school nearby. Jemmy Hope, the United Irishman, often took his wife Rose for a walk, through these streets.

This is also Huguenot country — the people who came from France with their fine skills and traditions. Their word was their bond — 'as honest as a Huguenot', a quality of integrity which fitted like a glove into this area. They were industrious people and built the Weavers Hall, beautiful houses, shops, schools, and churches. They taught the people of Dublin to weave silks, tabinets, and Irish poplin — the finest poplin in the world. By their diligence and hard work they set up a hive of industry throughout this part of Dublin, which thrived until England wiped it out because of its effect on her own similar industries, particularly Linen and Poplin.

The Huguenots also brought us the garden shears, several species of flowers, a florist club and our very first pineapples to Ward's Hill in the Liberties. Many of their graves are in Peter Street, Stephen's Green, and the old Cabbage Garden, which still exists opposite the gates of Kevin Street Garda Station. So let us salute the names of Le Bas, Lefroy, la Touche, le-Clerc, Le Fanu, Dufour, Ducros, D'Olier, Montfort, Fleury, Boileau, Saurins, Espinasses, and Bouhereau, the eminent physician from Rochelle who was the gifted Librarian of Marsh's Library.

All religions lived together in the Liberties — Quakers, Jews, Mrs. Smyly's Homes, Margaret Aylward's Convent of the Holy Faith, Nano Nagles' schools in Blackpitts, John Wesley on tour and Frank Duff who founded the Legion of Mary in Francis Street. Irish, English, Latin, Dutch, French and Italian languages were spoken around this area as well as another language the clergy did not know!

Gone! Gone forever is the old Coombe Hospital founded by Margaret Boyle in 1826.
It was demolished early in 1974.

St. Joseph's Night Refuge for homeless women and children, Brickfield Lane, Dublin. Founded by the Very Rev. Dr. Spratt, 1860.

Take a walk down the Coombe by Jemmy Hope's shop (No.8) and on to Margaret Boyle's old Coombe Hospital, at present being demolished, founded for the poor of Dublin. Go on to Ardee Street to Con Colbert's outpost in 1916, once Watkins' Brewery. Walk up to St. Joseph's Night Shelter which was the old Stove Tenter House founded by Thomas Pleasants for the poor weavers of the Liberties to help them dry their cloth in wet weather.

Fr. Spratt (Carmelite) born in Cork Street, 5th January 1796 turned the old empty stove house into a night shelter for poor women and children. Fr. Spratt was the man who found the ancient statue of Our Lady of Dublin which originally stood in St. Mary's Abbey. He also saved the ancient Lucky Stone which belonged to St. Audoen's Church. He was also responsible for getting the site in Whitefriar Street for the Carmelite Church. This site was where the first Carmelite church had stood in the 13th century.

THE LORD MAYOR'S LIBERTY

The Lord Mayor of Dublin was a bit browned-off *(fed up)* with Liberties. It seemed as if they were closing in on him, so a new term was used when referring to the city inside the walls of Dublin — the Lord Mayor's Liberty. The citizens within had the right of franchise, provided of course that they paid the fine of a pair of gloves to the Lord Mayor's wife. One Lord Mayor admitted so many people to the franchise that his wife was able to open a glove shop in Skinner's Row (Christchurch Place).

A citizen also had the liberty of standing with the Butter Boys and selling his products in the open markets of the city. The Trade Guilds were all in the city in the 14th and 15th century, and they had the liberty of fixing prices on their products. If anyone broke the rules they soon lost their liberties and ended up in prison or the Common Stock on Christchurch Hill. The citizens also enjoyed the protection of the city walls, guarded by the night watch. They could leave and enter again by the city gates without fear of being stopped by the city Beadles who manned the gates to keep strangers, swine, dogs and sheep out of the city.

They could also enjoy the voice of the good singing boy and the musicians who were employed by the Lord Mayor to entertain the people in the streets of Dublin. Now that was an excellent custom — why don't we have it today? A good ballad group walking around the streets playing music and singing 'Molly Malone', 'Biddy Mulligan', and 'Twenty Men from Dublin Town'.

The Lord Mayor and the City Fathers met in the Tholsel at Skinner's Row beside Ram Alley. On certain days of the year the Lord Mayor put a complete stop on all liberties, and ordered all citizens within and all other people without to come into the city and give a day's work free of charge to mend the pot-holes in the streets. If anyone refused to come, the watch (guard) was sent out to drag them in.

The city also had a Charter de Libertatum Civitatis Dublini from King John granting them lands on the northside (outside the walls) from St. Mary's Abbey to Clonliffe by the Tolka.

The Lord Mayor and City Fathers met in the Tholsel at Skinner's Row beside Ram Alley. This area is now callea Christchurch Place.

The Lord Mayor at one stage ordered all Pest Houses (Fever Hospitals) to be built outside the city walls, and a few men to be employed to look after the sick and bury the dead. He also appointed a Beadle to carry a long white forty-foot pole to walk in front of the sick on their way to the Pest House. This is where we get the saying (still common today) 'I wouldn't touch him with a forty-foot pole'.

Looking under the arch of Christchurch and down Winetavern Street towards the River Liffey.

LIBERTY OF CHRISTCHURCH

Poor Christchurch, sure they didn't get a look in at all. The bit of land from King John never brought them a halfpenny. And those fellows down the hill in St. Patrick's made life a terrible burden. Time and again they asked "What are we going to do, everyone has a liberty except us. We are the oldest cathedral (1038). We have right on our side, truth on our side, tradition on our side, and the markets on our side" (Fishamble Street) — "That's it", said the Prior, "the markets on our land, why didn't I think of that before".

"Let's go to the Tholsel and demand our liberty. Let us pray first. Let us now meditate". A few hours later they met in Council. "Well my brothers, shall we make our demands?" A wise voice answered. "Why not do it the other way? Let us lobby a few of the City Fathers, get them to make the demand on our behalf. The perfect idea, who will we approach first. I know an alderman who is a true friend of Christchurch." At the next meeting of the City Fathers the question was asked about Christchurch Cathedral.

Soon the gates of Fishamble were joined to the gates of Christchurch, and the Prior held the only key. Then a toll was levied to get in or get out. The Manor and Courts of Grangegorman (Manor Street) were started, and later still more lands were granted in Phibsboro and Glasnevin. Christchurch had its liberties at last. In fact they did very well indeed, they even had 'Dublin's Hell' and also Winetavern Street with its 137 ale-houses. The Prior hadn't to go far for a drop in those days.

The Provost of Trinity College Dublin told the students on more than one occasion that 'Dublin's Hell' was out of bounds and that he would expel anyone found there at night-time. 'Hell' was the site just beyond Christchurch Yard near St. Michael's Hill. It was a small area of taverns and bed-and-breakfast establishments in the Monto style. Robert Burns the poet wrote a few verses about Dublin's Hell. This place had nothing to do with 'The Four Corners of Hell'. In fact we really had eight corners of Hell. These were all pubs, the first four being Longford Street, Ship Street, Stephen's Street and Golden Lane, and the second four at Patrick Street, Dean Street, New Street and Kevin Street.

Christchurch Cathedral is worth a visit any day of the week. Go up and have a look at what is claimed to be the Tomb of Strongbow and his son, lying side-by-side. Visit the crypt, walk slowly around the chapels, kneel down on a pew, close your eyes and perhaps you will see Lambert Simnel (the imposter) sitting on a throne, and on his head the Golden Crown which was taken from the Virgin's Statue in the church of St. Maria del dam. He now claims to be King of Ireland and England (1487), having been proclaimed and crowned by the citizens of Dublin and the clergy of Christchurch Cathedral.

Open your eyes, stand up, look at your pew. Was that the pew that Laurence O'Toole knelt at when he was Archbishop? In the crypt you will find 'The Ancient Stocks', a relic of the old Liberties of Christchurch Cathedral.

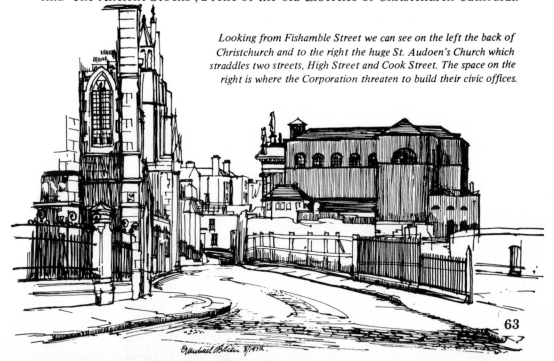

Looking from Fishamble Street we can see on the left the back of Christchurch and to the right the huge St. Audoen's Church which straddles two streets, High Street and Cook Street. The space on the right is where the Corporation threaten to build their civic offices.

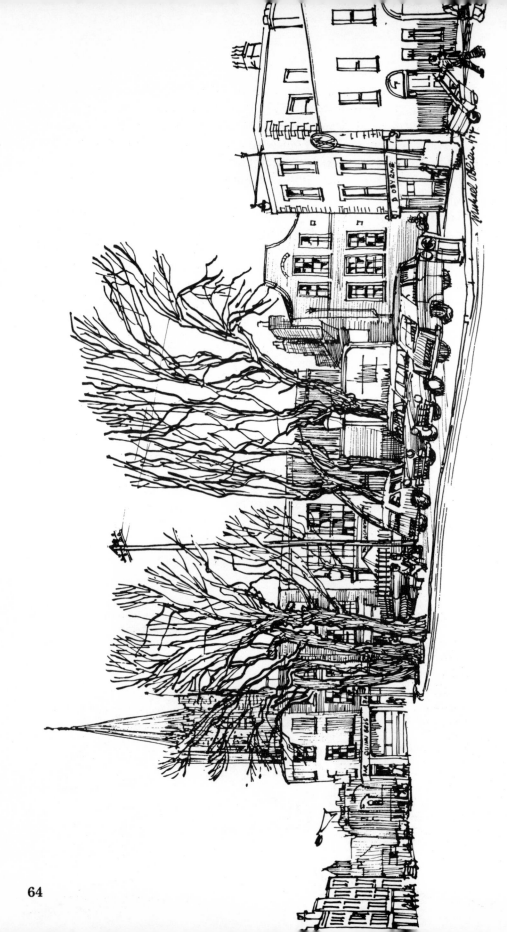

One of the Four Corners of Hell with a pub at each corner. This is where Patrick Street, Dean Street, New Street and Kevin Street meet. Many of the houses in the picture are in a bad state and will soon disappear. On the right is a very old Dutch Billy style house recently renovated.

CLONTARF

Clontarf, Cluain-Tarbh, Plain of the Bulls, a fitting name for all the bull the Vernons tried to pull in old Clontarf. In 1014 on a Good Friday morning King Brian fought the Danes and drove them into the sea near Conquer Hill. When the Anglo-Normans came Hugh De Lacy gave Clontarf to Adam De Phepoe. Adam built Clontarf Castle in 1175. On his death the castle and lands passed into the hands of The Knights Templar. In 1312 this order was suppressed and all their property passed to the Knights Hospitallers of St. John of Jerusalem. When this order was suppressed at the reformation, the castle and lands were given to the Prior John Rawson. He was created Viscount Clontarf because he handed over all the lands and property including the vast lands covering Kilmainham and the Phoenix Park. When Rawson died the lands became the property of the King.

In 1649 Oliver Cromwell divided Clontarf between his friends John Blackwell and John Vernon who was quarter-master-general of his army. Blackwell sold his interest to Vernon who was now lord and master of Clontarf Castle and lands. John Vernon was the grand-nephew of Sir George Vernon of Haddon in Derbyshire who was known as "King of the Peak".

The Vernons continued in possession and in the year 1731 there was a court action between the Vernons and the Dublin Corporation over Vernon's Liberty of Clontarf Island and the sea. Vernon claimed his Liberty, stating that the City's liberty boundary ended at Clonliffe Road. Cromwell had told the first Vernon that he could own the lands and sea as far as his eye could see. This Vernon claimed that he could see Liverpool on a fine day. The Vernons lost the court action and this gave Dublin Corporation the green light to move in on the other Liberties. Within 130 years they completed the job.

In the year 1650 the sand island of Clontarf was turned into a Pest House by the Lord Mayor of Dublin. Vernon did not object to this, in fact it seems as if Vernon had suggested it himself.

For many years a Captain Cromwell lived in a wooden house on Clontarf Island. His son Christopher had a publichouse in Beaver Street. After the captain died his son moved into the island house which was known as Cromwell's Court. On the night of a big storm, 9th October 1844 the wooden house was washed away, and Christopher Cromwell and his son William were both drowned.

Dr. Carmichael, the eminent Dublin surgeon and the founder of The School of Medicine in Peter Street, was drowned at Sutton Creek on 8th June 1849. He attempted to cross it on horseback from Dollymount to his residence at Sutton at low tide. The tomb of Carmichael is in St. George's Churchyard, Whitworth Road, a few yards from the tomb of Annie Hutton, the sweetheart of Thomas Osborne Davis. Annie Hutton's favourite place was Clontarf Island.

You can see that the Liberties spread to various parts of the city and county at different times. However, the old area around Christchurch and St. Patrick's is the area known today as 'The Liberties'.

Around St Werburghs

The outline of coffins and bones were caught in the beam of the sexton's lamp as we looked around the vaults of this ancient church. The earth was dry, and down the passage we walked to the end of the cell-like vault. There on the ground lay the black coffin, with a brass plate inscribed 'Lord Edward Fitzgerald'. This was the new coffin which his grand-daughter had purchased, and not the plain brown one that came from the Newgate Jail. We also looked for the remains of James Ware, but, looked in vain, for Lord Edward's coffin was the only one that was still intact.

Lord Edward Fitzgerald was buried in St. Werburgh's at dead of night. Only one mourner, Lady Louisa Connolly of Castletown House Celbridge, his aunt, followed the coffin. However, an old man witnessed the lonely funeral, recognised Lady Louisa, and knew that they were the remains of the rebel chief. Later that night he entered the vaults and found the plain brown coffin, and with a rusty nail scraped the initials 'E.F.'. Years later on his death-bed in High Street he related his story, and by so doing made the task of Lord Edward's grand-daughter easy when she came to Dublin to find her grand-father's grave. After the arrest of Lord Edward, his wife and children were sent into exile by Dublin Castle and never returned to Dublin.

We came up by the manhole type entrance, walked around the church-yard and past the grave of Mayor Sirr and then entered the church near the altar. I paused to examine the beautiful wooden pulpit. It was designed by Francis Johnston and carved by a skilled craftsman named Richard Stewart. Then I closely examined the large bell in the centre of the black and white tiled aisle. The bell tells its own story and originally came from the church of St. Bride. It has the name 'Napper Tandy' church warden on it.

Left — The lovely iron gates of St. Werburgh's Church in Werburgh Street.

Michael O'Brien 1977.

Above, on the balcony hangs the elaborate coat of arms of George III which along with the pulpit came from The Chapel Royal in Dublin Castle. The large windows would appear to assist the acoustics when the sweet notes of the organ flow gently in the air. Many fine musicians have recorded for radio in St. Werburgh's church, one I know claimed that the acoustics of St. Werburgh's were the finest in Dublin.

The original entrance facing Werburgh Street is not used, and in its hallway lies a 16th century Fitzgerald Tomb. Also to be seen is an interesting record which tells the price of a Muffed Funeral Bell in days gone by. By far the most striking feature in the hallway are two old wooden hand pump type 'fire engines'. The parish pumps of latter days, similar to the pumps manufactured by John Oats, who lived at the 'Sign of the Boot' in Dame Street. Oats claimed that he could manufacture 'Water Ingins' as good as any Londoner.

The entrance to the church today is a doorway in Bristol Buildings in Castle Street. The name Bristol is a reminder of the men and women who came from that city to take over Dublin 800 years ago. Castle Street is steeped in history. Here was the birthplace of James Ware, Historian and Antiquarian, and alongside was the Banking House of David de la Touche. Across the street was the house where Conor Maguire and Lord McMahon planned the 1641 Rising. The beautiful Rates Office was originally Newcomens Bank. Castle Street was also a hub of booksellers and publishers and also writers. Some of the finest books the street ever saw were those from the quills of James Ware and Duald Mac Fírbis. The latter was hired by Ware to translate The Register of Clonmacnoise and other Gaelic manuscripts. On one of his journeys to Sligo he was mysteriously murdered. After Ware's death his vast library and collection of translations and manuscripts went into the hands of Lord Clarendon — Dean Swift made an attempt to save them for Dublin but failed. The collection changed hands a few times but ended up in the British Museum under the name of the Clarendon Manuscripts.

Dean Swift was born in Hoey's Court nearby, and William Penn the founder of Pennsylvania lived for a while beside St. Werburgh's. Cromwell also stopped here as did many Quakers, Huguenots, and the first Dublin Lodge of the Orange Order.

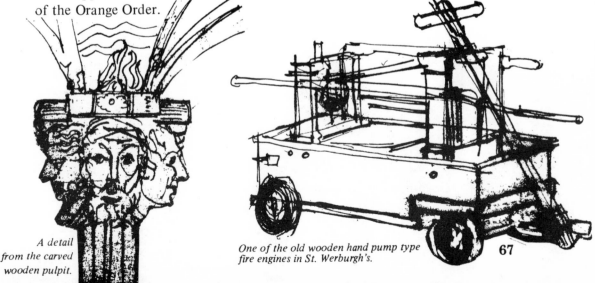

A detail from the carved wooden pulpit.

One of the old wooden hand pump type fire engines in St. Werburgh's.

Left – This illustration of about 1840 shows Dublin Castle, and in Castle Street, behind the lamp standard appears the La Touche Bank – for many years one of the leading banks in Dublin. The Rates Office on the right was previously the Hibernian Bank and before this Newcomens Bank.

Below – Castle Street today and the remains of the La Touche Bank.

The last wooden house in Dublin stood at the corner of Castle Street, near St. Werburgh's Church. The Rev. Nicholas Walsh who gave many years' service to St. Werburgh's was the man who first brought the Gaelic (Irish-type letters) for printing to Dublin in 1571, and down the street John Ogilvy founded the first theatre in 1635.

A most frequent visitor to Werburgh Street was Lady Morgan who passed by the church each evening on her way to the Queen's Head Tavern. They say that Lady Morgan started the tradition of bringing porter home in a milk jug. Did your granny ever send you to the pub for porter? Well, if she did, go up to Werburgh Street and you'll see the pub (now the Napper Tandy) where it all started.

St. Werburgh's was Lord Edward's favourite church, and its still very much with us, standing in the shadows between the birthplace of two Dublin poets – Swift and Mangan

Ford of Hurdles

From Butt Bridge at Liberty Hall to Sean Heuston Bridge near the C.I.E. Railway Station the River Liffey is spanned by nine bridges. The River Liffey divides the city north and south and is a great boon to tourists and strangers as all one has to do is keep to the Liffey Wall on either side, cross any bridge, keep your bearing, make your way back to the Liffey again and you will never get lost in Dublin.

Take a walk from O'Connell Bridge up along the quay. Pass the Ha'penny Bridge, or The Metal Bridge as it is sometimes called. After it was erected in 1816 it was called The Wellington Bridge — it got its name Ha'penny from the toll that had to be paid years ago to cross the Liffey at this spot. Today the bridge leads to the beautiful Irish tweeds' shop, and Hector Grey on Sunday mornings standing on his wooden throne selling his bargains in all kinds of merchandise. Hector is as much a part of Dublin as the Lord Mayor's chain.

Look across Capel Street Bridge and view the beautiful City Hall at the end of Parliament Street. It was originally designed and opened as a Royal Exchange, and its hard to credit that this was the site of public whipping and garroting up to the year 1815. Behind City Hall stands Dublin Castle, the only

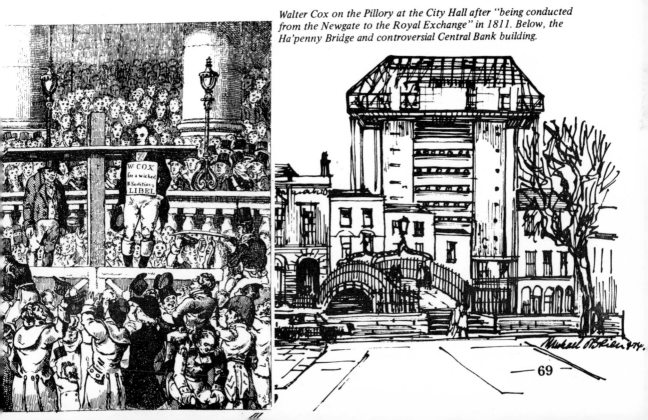

Walter Cox on the Pillory at the City Hall after "being conducted from the Newgate to the Royal Exchange" in 1811. Below, the Ha'penny Bridge and controversial Central Bank building.

Church Street Bridge on the site of Dublin's first bridge and the Ford of Hurdles.

castle in the world which doesn't look like a castle, but the State apartments and the Chapel Royal are worthy of your attention. This was the seat of British power in Ireland for nearly 800 years. Beyond Capel Street Bridge lies Winetavern Street Bridge and beyond that again is Church Street Bridge.

Wait! Stop! Go no further. Stand on Church Street Bridge, look in any direction, stand and think, you're in the footprints of St. Patrick — nay, you're in the footprints of The Donn of Cooley, you're in the footprints of Little John — no, not the one who got out of Mountjoy, but his precursor He was Robin Hood's friend, who came to Dublin from Sherwood Forest and shot an arrow from this bridge to the top of Church Street, to show his skill with the bow. Little John was hanged in the fields of Oxmanstown beyond the Blue Coat School, on the road to Arbour Hill. Church Street Bridge is at the Ford of Hurdles the first bridge built across the Liffey and the spot where Dublin gets one of its three Gaelic names, Baile Atha Cliath (Ford of Hurdles), Dubhlinne (Dark River Pool), Druim Cuill Coille (Hazelwood Ridge). Church Street Bridge, the Ford of Hurdles, is named Fr. Mathew Bridge — after the great Capuchin Temperance Priest.

I mentioned there The Donn of Cooley (from *The Táin*) — the great Ulster Bull defended by Cuchulain. Now I don't want to go into mythology, but we in Dublin (meself and me brother) believe that the bull came from the little green field beside Paddy Ennis's pig yard in the Liberties. The Ford of Hurdles, made of bundles of brushwood laid across the river enabled, among other things, the Ulster cattle raiders to get the herds across to the northern road. One of the five great roads from Tara crossed the Liffey at this spot. It was here around 448 that St. Patrick is reputed to have said that Dublin would grow to become the principal city of Ireland — so to honour our Four Green Fields, the Four Provinces of Ireland — Ulster, Munster, Leinster, and Connaught, make four short tours from the Ford of Hurdles. Use the drawing on page 72 as a guide, and remember if you get lost all you have to do is find your way back to the Liffey.

TOUR ONE — BRIDGE STREET

Stand on Church Street Bridge. Facing the city on your left is Church Street and on your right is Lr. Bridge Street. Take Bridge Street first. The vacant site on the corner was once the Dublin home of Rory O'Moore, leader of the 1641 Rising — "For God, Ireland and Rory O'Moore" was the battle cry in those days. A later member of the same family founded the Irish College in Rome, became chancellor of a few French universities and was the only non-Frenchman to be given the honour of delivering the commemoration address to celebrate the reign of Louis XIV. Still on vacant ground, on your left was the birthplace of Jimmy O'Dea. The Kosmo Bar covers part of James Mullet's tavern where the Invincibles used to meet. Mullet was chairman of the the Irish National Invincibles (1882) and spent about 12 years of his life in jail. Just beyond the Kosmo Publichouse a plaque marks the wall which was once the home of Oliver Bond. It was here that the Leinster Directory were arrested by Major Sirr on 12th March 1798. The password for the meeting was betrayed to Dublin Castle by Thomas Reynolds who was a member of the Directory — Major Sirr and his men knocked on the door, a voice answered "Who's there?". The Major shouted "Is Ivers from Carlow come". The door opened, arrests followed, and that evening the Leinster Directory (except Lord Edward Fitzgerald) were in chains in Newgate Jail.

Oliver Bond was later murdered in the prison yard at Newgate Jail. Across the road from the house of Bond is a small laneway which leads to The Brazen Head, the oldest tavern in Ireland — 1614. It could be said that revolution kept it in business and nearly put it out of business down the years. It was a meeting-place for Irish revolutionaries in 1798, 1803 (see Emmet's Desk), 1848, 1867, 1916 and in the Black and Tan days. After every rising it was raided. In 1916 it was almost destroyed and in 1922 when the Free State forces shelled the Four Courts garrison, the vibration of the heavy British artillery used shook the foundation of the Brazen Head.

At the top of Lr. Bridge Street stood the old Wormwood Gate and the steep hill straight ahead leads to Cornmarket, the birthplace of Napper Tandy (United Irishman). The famous ballad "The Wearin' of the Green" has the following verse —

I met with Napper Tandy and he took me by the hand
And said how's poor old Ireland and how does she stand.
She's the most distressful country that ever yet was seen
For they're hangin' men and women for the wearin' of the green.

Tandy's house at 21 Cornmarket was standing a few years ago, just around the corner on the left, at the top of the hill in High Street. If you look across

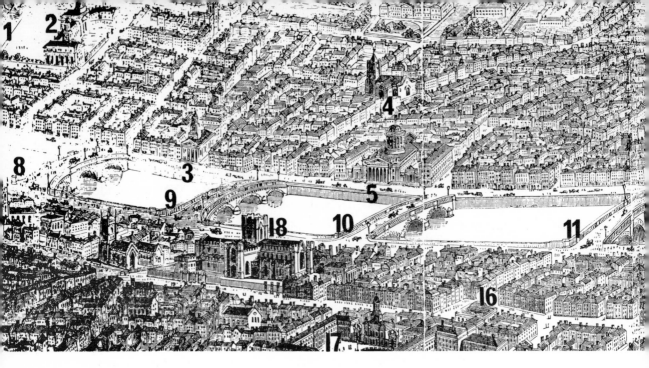

the road you will see the site of the first Newgate Jail and part of the old town wall which has been preserved. A few years ago the wall, with a gate entrance, ran the length of Lamb Alley. Standing at the wall you can see The Tailors' Hall, another treasure of Dublin. Before you make your way back to the Ford of Hurdles for the second tour take a good view of the green domes and the northern skyline.

TOUR TWO — OXMANTOWN AND DR. STEEVENS

This tour takes us along the quays towards the Phoenix Park. Number 12 **Arran Quay** was the birthplace of Edmund Burke, the golden orator whose statue stands outside Trinity College. Charles Halliday, author of "Scandinavian Kingdom of Dublin" had offices in Number 27. St. Paul's Church also on Arran Quay is very popular with Dublin people. It has a beautiful dome and pillars and was one of the first churches to ring out its peal of bells when Catholic Emancipation was granted (1829).

After this date a number of Italian marble workers came to Dublin to adorn Catholic Churches. Among these craftsmen was a man named Carsoni. His son became an architect and designed St. Peter's Church in Phibsboro. Carsoni's grandson was born in Harcourt Street and he too was named after his father "Edward". He was educated in Trinity College and later became Sir Edward Henry (1900). He was M.P. for Dublin University (Trinity) and a Bencher of the King's Inn Dublin. He helped found Carson's Volunteers to fight against Home Rule, and he also worked to establish the Six County Parliament (Stormont).

The next bridge at Queen Street (officially called Queen Maev Bridge) leads to The Hay Market, Coopers, the horse dealers (one of the last remaining in Dublin) and also Thundercut Alley and the streets to Grangegorman. The

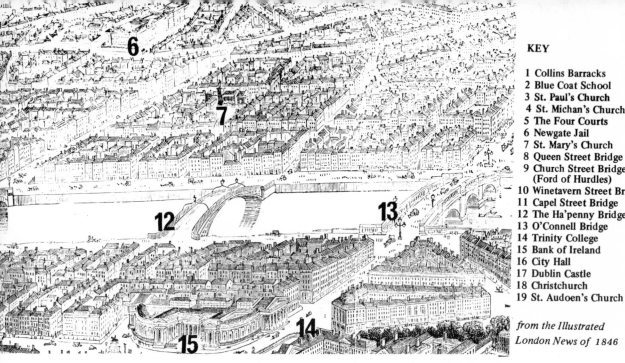

KEY

1 Collins Barracks
2 Blue Coat School
3 St. Paul's Church
4 St. Michan's Church
5 The Four Courts
6 Newgate Jail
7 St. Mary's Church
8 Queen Street Bridge
9 Church Street Bridge
   (Ford of Hurdles)
10 Winetavern Street Bridg
11 Capel Street Bridge
12 The Ha'penny Bridge
13 O'Connell Bridge
14 Trinity College
15 Bank of Ireland
16 City Hall
17 Dublin Castle
18 Christchurch
19 St. Audoen's Church

*from the Illustrated
London News of 1846*

turn on your right after Queen Street Bridge leads to the old Blue Coat School buildings and the road to Arbour Hill and the graves of the executed leaders of the 1916 Easter Week Rising.

*Right — the twisting mediaeval shape of Back Lane and the Tailors Hall.
Below — the entrance gate to the Tailors Hall.*

The **Blue Coat School** was designed by a Corkman — Thomas Ivory, who left us a few gems of Georgian buildings in Dublin. The school got its name from the strange dress of its pupils. The schoolboys wore blue uniforms — they must have been a colourful sight on the streets of Dublin. A dark blue cut-away coat, brass buttons, yellow waistcoats, dark blue knee breeches, yellow stockings and silver buckle shoes. Down the times the uniform changed in style, but never in colour and even when the school governors decided to do away with the uniform in 1923 they replaced it with a blue serge suit.

The old Blue Coat building, "The Hospital and Free School of King Charles II" at Oxmantown, commonly called King's Hospital or Blue Coats, was first founded in 1669 in Queen Street by the Dublin Corporation. A year later King Charles II granted them a Royal Charter — the Queen Street school-house was once used by the Irish Parliament in 1729. The school in Blackhall Place dates from 1784. The new King's Hospital School is at Brooklawn in Palmerstown. A merger has taken place between Morgan House Junior School, Mercers' Girls' School and The King's Hospital.

As you continue up the quay beyond Blackhall Place you are coming into "truck driver country" where a large number of country truck drivers 'drum up' (get their meals) dinners and teas before heading in and out of Dublin. The area is noted for a number of neat and tidy and reasonably-priced restaurants and cafes. If its a ball of malt or a few pints you need, well there are a number to choose from, between The Bark Kitchen and Ryan's beautiful Victorian Bar at Parkgate Street.

As you reach Sarsfield Quay, stop and look through the railings — yes, I know its a shame, sheep grazing and football pitches on the graves of our heroic dead. This is The Croppies Hole. What was it that Dr. Madden (author of *Lives and Times of United Irishmen*) said? Oh yes — "Someday this land will

be consecrated and men and women will come with funeral trophies in honour of the noble dead of 1798". Well its now 1974 and they haven't come yet to the graves of Lawless, Esmonds, Teeling, Tone (Matthew, a brother of Wolfe Tone) and the countless other forgotten names who lie here in a mass grave.

Collins Barracks in the high background was the old Royal Barracks, the first built in Dublin, where Kipling was inspired to write his Barrack Room Ballad. At the rear of the barracks was the old Provost Prison where Wolfe Tone was murdered (1798). Cross over the next bridge (Sean Heuston) and as you do so note the fine structure on your right. Its the headquarters of C.I.E. standing in front of the railway station. If you look straight ahead you will see the Nurses' Home of Dr. Steevens Hospital and if you walk up the lane by the side of the Home you will soon see the hospital itself. It dates from 1720 and is the second oldest in Dublin. The hospital courtyard is most unusual and is well worth a visit. As a tribute to all the great hospitals of Dublin, and to the dedicated service of doctors, nurses and staff, I would like to record the name of the late Dr. Oliver Chance, one of the greatest skin specialists of Europe, who attended the poor of Dublin for many years in Dr. Steevens and other city hospitals. In the year 1936, Monday, Wednesday and Friday— he manned the outpatients dispensary with kindness, courtesy and above all dignity. Pay your shilling on a Friday and if you could not pay, the lady almoner (treasurer) just smiled and said don't worry about it.

Above the hill from the hospital gate stands Dean Swift's (St. Patrick's Hospital). Visitors are welcome to visit the Swift Museum in the entrance hall. You had better go back to the bridge on the Liffey. I don't want you to get lost at Bow Lane, The Forty Steps or the Robbers' Den. As you walk down the south side of the Liffey you will pass Guinness's Brewery on your right. The old jetty on the river-side is gone. Sure the Liffey isn't the same at all at all since they took down the jetty and got rid of the barges.

The bridge at the corner of Watling Street was known in olden days, as Bloody Bridge. No, it had nothing to do with Ireland's fight for freedom, but with the fight for freedom of the Liffey. This was a ferry crossing and

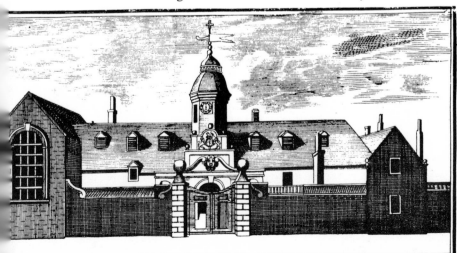

BLUE COAT BOYS HOSPITAL

Left – The old Blue Coat School which was founded in 1669 and stood in Queen Street, opposite the present building illustrated on the opposite page. This fine building which is in Blackhall Place is now owned by the Incorporated Law Society and at present lies empty and disused.

when the bridge was built, the ferrymen caused a riot, because as they said it was, " Taking the bread out of our mouths". Beyond the bridge is Usher's Island. Number 20, which was standing a few years ago is gone. It was the home of Francis Magan, the man who informed on Lord Edward Fitzgerald. This did not come to light until several years after Magan's death. However, his sister, Mary, knew that he was the informer. It nearly drove her insane and she never left the house, and lived like a recluse for over forty years. Some historians have stated that it was Mary Magan's life that inspired Charles Dickens to write his book *Great Expectations.*

Only the gate posts remain of The Mendicity Institution. It was once the home of Lord and Lady Moira. Moira House 'The most beautiful in Europe' said John Wesley, was the place Lord Edward's family lived before being deported to England after Lord Edward's death in Newgate Jail in 1798. Moira House became The Mendicity Institution for Paupers in 1828. The Mendicity Institution was an outpost of the G.P.O. garrison in 1916. It was under the command of Sean Heuston, who was later executed. In his last letter to his sister, a Dominican nun, he said "If you really love me, teach the children the history of Ireland".

Usher's Island leads onto Usher's Quay. Numbers 18 to 20 are occupied by Ganly's Auctioneers, Wool Brokers, Land Agents and Livestock Salesmen. The premises covers the site where the Quakers lived in their community circle in the last century. The Quakers, like the Huguenots, were always noted for their honest dealings and their Meeting House stands today at Number 6 Eustace Street where they have been for over half-a-century. The history of this noble community in Dublin would justify close study.

TOUR THREE – THE BRIDEWELL AND ST. MICHAN'S

As you cross the Ford of Hurdles Bridge, straight ahead is Church Street. The Four Courts Hotel which closed in 1974, was once the old Angel Inn dating back to the late 17th century. The first turn on the left is Hammond Lane, the word Hammond being a corruption of Hangman's Lane which in the 16th century led to the common hanging grounds of Oxmantown Woods. The first turn on the right leads to The Bridewell cells and old Pill Lane (Chancery Street). Visitors are not welcome in the Bridewell, unless of course, you have a prior reservation. If that be the case, you will check in at the desk, give your name and address, leave all your luggage, razor blades, shoe laces etc. in the cloakroom, and climb the stone stairway to your private room, a filthy hole, a hair mattress bed in lumps like the Three Rock Mountains and Kippure, a brown stained wall around a corner open stone toilet bowl, two dirty blankets a dirty pillow filled with rocks I think.

Remember what Oliver St. John Gogarty said about Joyce's book *Ulysses*? Well, if Gogarty had ever been in the Bridewell, he would have said that Joyce wrote it here. The cell walls tell their own story: Johnny Loves Mary;

names, dates, sex talk, football teams, up Bohs, shag Rovers; threats to the Judge, the Fuzz, the Cops, poems, dirty jokes, the Red Flag Chairman Mao, X's and O's.

"I'll never steal again, I'm very sorry, no I'll never steal again" under which was written "Cut out the bloody moaning and do your time — and make sure they don't catch you next time out" — "Good luck Joey and Mona, and Frankie Reilly slept here". During the night, you get out of bed a few times for a rest. The toilet chain is outside the cell door, in case you hang yourself with it. In the morning the charlady shouts in the spy-hole — "Son, Son, do you want your chain pulled? Son, will I pull your chain Son?" But lately the Bridewell have gone all modern, but only in relation to the toilet chain — the rest remains the same but the charlady is missing and a computer press-button system in a downstairs office flushes all the cell toilets in one go.

The street outside the Bridewell door leads to the old Pill Lane and it may be of interest to the Dublin branch of Women's Lib, that King Charles I in 1641 signed and sealed a Royal Charter which granted to all citizens of Dublin "The Pill" and the charter also said that "The Pill" was for their childer and their childers' childer for ever and ever amen. In fact the 'Pill' was a name given

The back yard of the Bridewell and the stone tower of St. Michael's Church.

77

to a miniature harbour and this harbour was used by St. Mary's Abbey and various traders over the centuries. This was years before the Liffey quay walls were built.

Millars Dublin Copper and Brass Works is an old established company; part of their premises covers the site of the house of Henry Jackson (United Irishman) who had an iron foundry here in 1776. His daughter, Eleanor, born at this spot, became the wife of Oliver Bond. Eleanor was also a member of The United Irishmen and administered The United Irishmen Oath to several distinguished Dublin recruits. After Oliver Bond's death, Eleanor and the children emigrated to America — she returned to Dublin about the year 1820 to unveil a statue to her father. Eleanor herself lived to a ripe old age and she is buried in Boston, U.S.A.

Across the road stands St. Michan's Church, pronounced by Dubliners as 'Saint Mick-anns'. This church founded in 1095 is steeped in history. Go in and visit the vaults and graveyard. See the baptismal font where the waters were poured on the heads of Eleanor Bond and Edmund Burke. Sit on the stool of repentance, the only one in Dublin. Note the pulpit, the altar rail, the fine wood carving on the front of the organ gallery. This was Parnell's favourite Dublin church. If you hear the organ playing and yet see no one at it, it might be the ghost of Handel back again to play another tune before going to The Fishamble Street Music Hall to perform for the first time his famous *Messiah* — April 1742.

The vaults of St. Michan's contain the coffins of the Shears brothers who died side by side on the scaffold outside Newgate Jail in 1798. In the graveyard seek out the graves of Oliver Bond, Dr. Charles Lucas and The Rev. Mr. Jackson. Place a flower on their clay, for these three men loved Ireland and should always be remembered and honoured.

Your next stop as you walk up Church Street must be the Capuchin Friary. The first names that spring to mind are Albert and Dominick, Columbus, Sebastian, Aloysius and Augustine — all friars who were deeply involved in the Irish struggle for freedom, from 1916 to 1923. Their lives and deeds would fill many volumes — from the bullet-swept streets of Dublin with Elizabeth O'Farrell and Pearse's surrender order, to the execution yard in Kilmainham Jail and to exile and pain in far off lands. Both Fr. Albert Bibby and Fr. Dominick O'Connor were sent into exile in 1924. Within ten months Fr. Albert was dead. His last dying request was that his body should rest on Irish soil — "Let me rest with Liam, Rory and the boys in Glasnevin". He died on February 14th 1925 at Santa Barbara, California, U.S.A.

Beyond the Capuchin Friary is the Father Mathew Hall where the annual Feis Ceoil is held. Here the little children of Dublin dance and sing, recite, act and speak verse in competition for silver cups and medals. At the cross-roads was Reilly's Fort, an outpost of the 1916 Rising. On the far side of the road in front of the new flats, Kevin Barry was arrested in 1920. As you walk up the hill the first turn on your left leads to the old Channell Row

Convent site, which was founded in the year 1717 by the six foundresses of the Dominican Order of nuns – Mary Bellew, Julia Brown, Ellen Keating, Alice Rice, Elizabeth Weaver and Honora Vaughan. In 1819 the sisters moved to their present site at Cabra and are continuing in the same tradition that started in Channell Row.

The fine building running along North Brunswick Street with the many small green domes is the main front of the Richmond Hospital. It is now joined to the Hardwicke and Whitworth Hospitals. These were known as the House of Industry Hospitals and covered the land of the Ancient House of Industry, later known as The North Dublin Union. This was the first workhouse built in Dublin in the late 17th century.

Near the top of Constitution Hill is the old Broadstone Railway Station, now a bus depot. Across the road behind the high iron railings is the large impressive building known as The King's Inns. The present building dates from 1800 and covers part of Lord Mountjoy's land (that man again!). The area was once known as Primate's Hill and leads to Henrietta Street by a small arch-type gateway at the rere of the building to where Lord Mountjoy had one of his town houses. The King's Inn Library was erected in 1827 at a cost of £20,000. The Library contained over 100,000 volumes of books dealing with legal and historical matters and a wide range of books on Dublin's history. It seems that The King's Benchers were more concerned with eating food than drinking knowledge, as their dining hall cost £45,000 and since 1822 considerable sums have been spent on repairs and decorations. In 1973 The Benchers sold by

The front of the Richmond Hospital in North Brunswick Street.

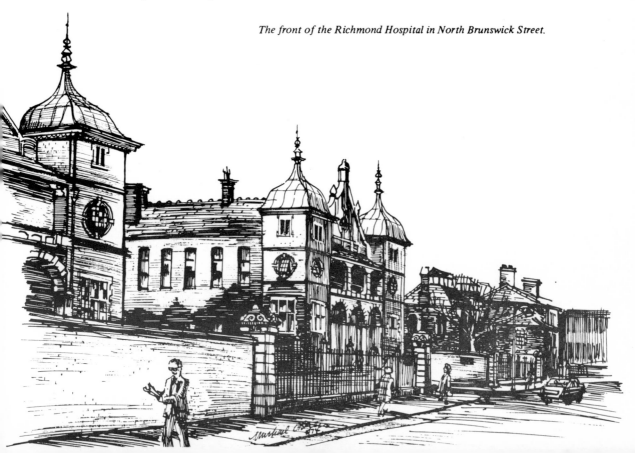

Henrietta Street showing the back entrance to The King's Inns and to the left of the street is the Law Library. The medal on the left shows the front view of the King's Inns.

auction in London many priceless books from the Library. Some of these were rescued by An Taisce, who bought at the auction various rare items relating to Ireland.

During the 1798 Rising five members of The King's Inns were "struck from the rolls forever" for the part they played in the ranks of The United Irishmen. On your way back down the Hill to the Ford of Hurdles for the fourth and final tour, watch out for a horseman riding fast — it may be King James running away from the Battle of the Boyne. When James reached Dublin Castle (1690) he stated "The cowardly Irish ran away and left me" — but the lady at the Castle gate answered quickly "It seems that your Majesty has won the race".

TOUR FOUR – MERCHANT'S QUAY AND THE FOUR COURTS

This tour starts across The Ford of Hurdles and down Merchant's Quay. On the far side of the Liffey stands Gandon's Four Courts. This is the best spot from which to admire the fine building with its green dome and bullet-scarred pillars. June 28th 1922 and Civil War — Rory O'Connor, Liam Mellows, Dick Barrett and Joe McKelvey of the Republican Forces, and the scribbled note from Fr. Albert Bibby O.F.M. Cap. "I was hearing confessions from 1 a.m. to 11 p.m., non-stop..." Fr. Albert's mind must have flashed back to the execution yard in Kilmainham Jail as he stood a few paces from Sean Heuston in 1916, and to the scaffold in Mountjoy Jail as he stood beside Kevin Barry in November 1920; or perhaps he wondered whose grave or whose execution would be next. Within ten days it will be Cathal Brugha's grave in Glasnevin — within four months he will be denied a last visit with Erskine Childers. Rory O'Connor, Liam Mellows, Dick Barrett and Joe McKelvey were taken prisoners at the Four Courts and were to die as a Free State reprisal on 8th December 1922.

The Four Courts stands on ancient lands where the Dominican Friars built their Abbey in the year 1224, three years after the death of St. Dominick. For many years they had a toll chapel on The Ford of Hurdles. The history of the Dominicans in Dublin is a long and chequered one. In 1539 the Prior of St. Saviours, Patrick Hay, surrendered the monastery to King Henry VIII. Three years later the lands were handed over to The Chancellor, John Allen and the Lord Chief Justice and other professors of law.

The Inns of Court were established, and here The Benchers had their rooms, meals and books, until they moved to The King's Inns. The Four Courts remained, and what are they called — The District? The Circuit? The Supreme? The High? The building contains in fact, The Courts of Chancery, King's Bench, Common Pleas and Exchequer — and if you are caught with no light on your bike you could end up in one of them. These terms are not of course used today and there are now eleven courts within the 'Four Courts' complex.

As you turn your eyes back to Merchant's Quay, remember that in The Four Courts' attack of 1922 the Records Office was completely destroyed by fire. This office contained several rare documents and manuscripts, relating to the early history of Dublin and Ireland. It also contained the early records of St. Michan's Church and many other parishes which had been transferred to The Four Courts for safety.

Merchant's Quay gets its name from the hive of Merchants, many of whom had their own vessels 200 years ago. In fact, up to about thirty years ago the side entrance to Adam & Eve's Church was known as Skippers Alley—

The Four Courts and Winetavern Street Bridge from Wood Quay

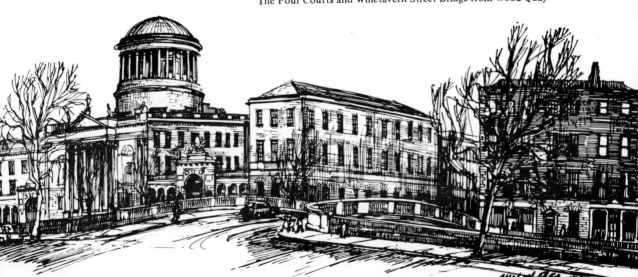

it would appear that this alley was reserved for the skippers and masters of the many vessels, native and foreign, that sailed up the Liffey's waters.

Adam & Eve's Church (The Franciscan Friary) gets its name from the old Adam & Eve's Tavern which was used as a Mass House during penal days The two St. Anthony's Halls beside the church are noted for concerts, carpet sales and bingo numbers. The Church has a fine Library Bookshop and Repository. If you walk down the park between the church and hall, it will lead you out to Cook Street, the street of the cooks, which was noted for good food, taverns by the score, and churches by the half-dozen. It once held five Order churches and many Mass Houses. This was also the hub of the printing industry in Dublin and they were fond of using colourful names such as The Sign of the Bible, The Sign of the Angel, The Sign of Dr. Hay's Head (Bridge Street corner). Those in the printing industry today are familiar with the term— "Father of the Chapel". I wonder does this term date back to the Cook Street printers who in those 17th century days printed prayer books and prayer leaflets for the chapels of Dublin.

Conor Maguire and Lord McMahon were arrested in 1641 where the Modern Schools stand today. They were later executed in Tyburn, England. Facing the school is the true gem of Dublin, the only remaining gateway in the old city walls — St. Audoen's, Arch. It was one of the first gates erected in the Danish stronghold of Dublin after the Battle of Clontarf in 1014. Only part of the old city wall remains — climb the steps slowly, listen — this is the spot where you can feel the heart of old Dublin — don't rush, take your time — you are in footprints of Ailred the Dane, going home to Newgate to start his hospital,

The square tower belongs to old St. Audoen's, Dublin's oldest parish church. It is here that you can descend the steps to pass under St. Audoen's Arch. The Four Courts appears in the picture.

and the noble tradition of the Augustinian Order in old John's Lane.

The Church (St. Audoen's) is a must for a visit. Three of its six bells are dated 1423 and are the oldest in Ireland. Call in and see the silver plate, touch the lucky or blessed stone in the hallway, and sense the spirits of hundreds and hundreds of years of history. The top of the steps leads to High Street, or Main Street Dublin, which dates back to the year 120 when Conn of the Hundred Battles and King Mogh of Munster divided Ireland between them and made High Street the border-line of the two kingdoms.

Turn to your left, walk down to the new St. Audoen's Church and then Christchurch Cathedral. You will pass the site of the house where Wolfe Tone's body was waked in 1798. The Cathedral dates from 1038 and its history is long and colourful. Go down under the archway of Christchurch into Winetavern Street and you will find yourself back at the Liffey Wall. On your right-hand-side is Viking Dublin where Mr. Breandan O'Riordan and his team from the National Museum found priceless treasures of Viking days dating back to the 9th century.

Beyond the vacant site lies St. Michael's and John's Church, and what was once the Fishamble Street Music Hall where Handel first performed his *Messiah* on 13th April 1742. The rere of the church stands where the old Smock Alley Theatre stood, and it was here that Peg Woffington made her name as she performed in the *Beggars Opera.* During the interval, Peg came out into the street to help her mother sell apples and oranges to the crowd from the gallery and the pit. Look back at Christchurch Cathedral and tell the Dublin Corporation to erect their offices somewhere else!

High Street, once the main street of Dublin is a sad sight today, most of the houses have been demolished. The front of St. Audoen's Church appears in the drawing.

Commercial Life

Back of the Pipes

Where are we going to hide our school-bags? What about the Robbers Den, or the tunnels in the Brickfields? No the last time we hid them there we couldn't remember which tunnel we put them in. How about 'the back of the pipes' — we were on the mitch from school so off we went down to the back of the pipes to hide our bags.

The same question was asked by the City Fathers in 1638. How about the back of the pipes — well, what about them? They are leaking, these pipes I mean. What do you want me to do, you're the Lord Mayor, you decide. But the people will soon have no water. The Lord Mayor decided, send a man to London for five tons of lead and a plumber.

Three weeks later the lead and two plumbers arrived. The work started at the back of the pipes on a site of land known as Lowsie Hill pronounced *Lousy Hill* by Dubliners. The plumbers repaired the pipes and advised the Corpo that yer man at the top of Lowsie Hill, the brewer named Giles Mee had too much of a draw off the city pipes, and if he didn't look after the back of the pipes the city would have no water. Mee who was also a city Alderman did not want to lose his brewery, so he looked after the back of the pipes.

After his death the brewery was given to his son-in-law, another Alderman, and later Lord Mayor of Dublin, Sir Mark Rainsford. He too left his name on one of our streets. He even opened up a theatre on Lowsie Hill, but it was a flop as the people of Dublin said it was too far out of the city.

Grand Canal Harbour, for many years used by Guinness's barges. It connects with the main line at Inchicore. Recently it was suggested that the harbour should be cleaned up and used for recreation purposes.

St, James's Gate, the main entrance to Guinness's Brewery was part of Mark Rainsford's Brewery. The house on the left, No.1 Thomas Street, is where the 'first Arthur' lived after he bought the brewery.

The brewery was now being run by Rainsford's son, also named Mark, and he rented it to a Huguenot named Paul Espinasse. That was in the year 1750 and Espinasse was later killed by a fall off his horse near the Black Bull Inn at Drogheda.

The Corpo had the brewery for a few years, and a couple of others tried to keep it going over the years. About this time Arthur Guinness was in Wales looking for a suitable place to start a brewery. Thanks be to God he couldn't find one. He came home to Dublin, and went for a walk up to the back of the pipes. He saw the empty brewery on Lowsie Hill, found the owner Mark Rainsford, and in 1759 did a deal and got the lot, lock stock and barrel, for a lease of 9,000 years at a rent of £45 a year. Isn't it a nice thought to know that you'll be able to drink Guinness for the next 8,785 years!

If I can take a liberty to say it, Dublin is a great city for drink and religion. You'll never run short of a pub or a church in Dublin. We have two and a half Cathedrals, and wasn't someone going to build another one at Merrion Square, and now I hear we are going to get another half cathedral in Westland Row. It was Roe's Whiskey that put the roof on Christchurch and Guinness's porter that saved St. Patrick's Cathedral, and will save it again for the city and the nation.

Sure doesn't drink and religion go hand in hand – God's first miracle didn't change the water into lemonade! No it was wine, and a good drop too, I believe. And didn't St. Patrick have his chief brewer Mescan by his side when he came to Dublin in 448. In the year 1610 we had 91 breweries, and 1180 ale houses, and 39 chapels and churches in Dublin.

It was the Archbishop of Cashel, Dr. Price, who started Arthur Guinness at beer-making. Arthur's father was an Estate Agent for the Bishop, and he often made a few buckets of table beer. The Bishop liked his drop, but soon learned that young Arthur made a superior bucket of brew. The praise went to young Arthur's head, and as soon as he grew up he started the business.

The waters for Guinness come from a spring in County Kildare named St. James's Well. Another well under Guinness's is used for cooling purposes. Remember the recipe — malt hops yeast and water — and you too might build the largest brewery in the world. But until that day comes you can still see one of the wonders of the world, the brewery of Arthur Guinness standing on Lowsie Hill at the back of the pipes. The pipes came along by Dolphin's Barn, down the laneway beside Maryland and the canal (where we hid our school-bags) around by the canal, and out into Thomas Street via Crane Street.

Within a stone's throw of the pipes was Marrowbone Distillery where Ceannt and McDonagh had a meeting before they decided on surrender in 1916. Marrowbone Lane was an outpost to the South Dublin Union garrison which was just across the canal. Marrowbone Lane also has the distinction of being the place where Charles Cameron started his free sulphur depot for the poor of Dublin. Cameron was the city's Medical Officer and made many changes during his long term with the Dublin Corporation. Sulphur was an expensive product, which only the rich could buy in time of fever. A sulphur bath hot or cold was three shillings, which was equal to three weeks' pay for a labourer in those dark Victorian days. Sulphur and the free disinfecting systems soon checked the outbreaks of fevers in Dublin.

If you ask a religious Dubliner how to get from Dame Street to the back of the pipes the answer will be "Go up by Christchurch, don't turn the hill to St. Patrick's, keep on by the new St. Audoen's church and the old St. Audoen's church, go on by John's Lane church to St. Catherine's church, and turn left before you come to St. James's church. You can't miss St. James's church its nearly facing the other St. James's church on the far side. — You're welcome and God bless ye".

If you ask a drinking man the same question the answer will be — "Go up past The Stag's Head, don't turn the corner to the Long Hall. Go on by Murty Lennon's up past The Lord Edward. Don't go down the hill to the Brazen Head and the Kosmo, but on up by Ryan's clock, and take the first turn on your left after you pass The Limelight. That sir will take you to the back of the pipes. You're welcome sir, and they all shut at eleven!"

Henry Grattan once said that he regarded the brewery at the back of the pipes (Guinness's) as "the actual nurse of the people and entitled to every encouragement, favour, and exemption". Maybe we could look for a liberty to take tax off Porter because after all, Porter first saw the light of day in Dublin's First Liberty in the Abbot's garden at the back of the pipes.

Merchants and Markets

"October 1870 Mr. and Mrs. A. Cameron, 73 Grafton Street Dublin, beg to announce their return from the markets and the arrival of their new goods, the latest fashions in millinery, mantles and dress materials, and call particular attention to a lot of sealskin mantles and black and coloured silks purchased considerably under price."

I doubt very much if the Camerons when they published this notice, had been to The Daisy, Iveagh, Norfolk or Patrick Street markets. Dublin City has always been a great centre for markets, merchants and traders of all kinds. It would be impossible to list all the interesting ones, so you'll forgive me if I only pick a select few.

The firm of John G. Rathborne Ltd., East Wall Road, Dublin 3 is the oldest firm in Dublin, dating back in tradition to the year 1488. The Rathborne family came to Dublin from Chester. The firm itself claims the year 1488 but I would like to think that the Rathborne s were in Ireland centuries before this date and its possible that some of them were in Dublin when the Foundation Stone of St. Werburgh's Church was laid in the 13th century. In Chester today stands the cathedral which was at one time the Abbey of St. Werburgh. So its most likely that the men of Chester had some influence in having a church in Dublin bearing the name Werburgh.

The firm of Rathborne's are Manufacturers in Wax and Spermaceti Candles. In the mid 13th century candle making was confined to rich and private houses, many of whom used beeswax from their honey hives. Mutton fat was also an expensive product. The poor used Rush-Lights. The Rathborne s

One of the few remaining old bicycle repair shops. Situated on the Phibsboro Road it overlooks the Royal Canal at Cross Guns Bridge.

by their method and ways of making candles made them available to the poor as well as the rich. How many times have you heard the expression "You could not hold a candle to it" — meaning that its beautiful and its the very best. This expression gives a fair idea of the high esteem in which candles were held.

The Rathbornes started business inside the old city walls near St. Werburgh's Church. Down the centuries they moved their premises to several places which included St. Mary's Abbey, Stoneybatter, Parnell Street and East Wall, also Essex Street. It seems that in each generation the family moved from premises to premises or street to street. A letter in the firm's files today, reveals that at one time in the 1840's the firm was a little short of capital and this was provided on loan by Rev. Thos. Luby D.D. Fellow, Trinity College, Dublin, who was married to Jane Rathborne. Church candles are still made in the same fashion as they were centuries ago. For special reasons church candles are made of bees' wax.

I don't think there is a house or room in Dublin which hasn't got a candle or maybe a half-a-candle. The next time the lights fail and you search for your spare candle, remember John Rathborne, the man who brought candles within the reach of the poor of Dublin for centuries.

One of the greatest merchants Dublin ever had was Daniel Maguire, who had his own Rope Manufacturing Company in Blackpitts in the Liberties, about 1798. He exported his products to Germany, Russia and Poland in his own vessels. This historic fact would never have been known, but for his letter in 1803 to Major Sirr telling about his sixteen year old son, who was a prisoner in the provost jail. The original letter is in the Sirr collection of papers and letters in Trinity College. Daniel Maguire lived beside his rope works on the site of ground known as 'ropers rest' a favourite haunt of Robert Emmet. He also had a house in Francis Street.

Goodbody's cigarette factory in Granville Place, was the first tobacco factory in Dublin. Mr. Goodbody moved from Tullamore, Co. Offaly to Blackpitts. At one time he grew his own tobacco, and had over 200 girls employed hand-rolling cigarettes.

Dolphin's Barn Brick Works was another old firm. It was situated at the first lock on the Grand Canal. Its rival was Hunter's of Corporation Street, who sold Newry Bricks. William Hunter sold these bricks all over Dublin and Ireland. Hunter's proudly advertised the quality of their product as follows:-

"Granite Sand, carried down the streams from the Mourne mountains, forms the main portion of the material from which our Bricks are made, and anyone with a rudimentary knowledge of chemistry knows this is an almost indestructible substance by either heat, cold, acids, or alkalies. It is fused by the action of intense heat and chemical action of lime, etc., into a Solid Pressed and Panelled and Facing Brick".

Over
E &

field in North King Street an old entrance of old firm still trading in this area.

LATE CLUB-HOUSE,
NO 35. COLLEGE GREEN.
Opposite the Bank of Ireland:

THIS NEW ESTABLISHMENT,
OPENED BY
RICHARD READ & CO.

WITHOUT arresting Public attention by any pompous Advertisement of Stock, or exaggerated advantages in price or superiority of Articles, has received that portion of public favour, which is the best evidence of the real benefits offered by them to their Friends and the Public to whom they pledge themselves, that no House in this City can have superior advantages in the selection of their Stock, better supplied, or on more interesting terms, in price or quality.

Those who have not yet made trial of their Stores, are particularly invited so to do, when they will meet every kind attention and encouragement. They can neither deserve or hope to retain a preference longer than they make it the interest of those who favour them with their commands.

TEAS

Of every description, and best characters—they will persevere in disposing of them on the low terms, which has already claimed such considerable attention

It is not possible that any House in this Country could have an advantage over them in the Importation of their Teas from the Honourable East India Company—*and they are determined not to be undersold.*

As an encouragement to Retailers, five pounds and upwards at same Price as by the Chest.

VERY OLD MALT WHISKEY.
WINES

Of every description, will be found very superior. *Smallest quantity Sold on trial*—FIVE dozen and upwards, same price as in Wood, save expense of bottling.

SUGARS, SPICES, and GROCERIES

Of all kinds, will be Sold on terms unusually low.

EAST and WEST INDIA PORTER, ALES
AND CIDER,

In high condition in Bottle.

The advertisement of 1819 speaks for itself.

89

*A newspaper advertisement of 1786 and right
a recent photo of a street trader.*

How could you beat that? Sure its no wonder The Dolphin Brick Works closed down.

Telford and Telford were the organ builders who supplied organs to dozens of churches and cathedrals in Ireland. It was Telford's who found the mummified remains of a cat and mouse in the organ of Christchurch Cathedral. You can see them both today in the crypt of Christchurch.

The Dublin Pure Ice Company did a roaring trade before the electric fridge was invented. The ice lollies today are nothing compared to a silver lump of pure Dublin ice.

The charcoal makers were in Cuffe Lane, headed by Daniel Mahar. Do you remember the charcoal-driven motor vans during the last war, or was yours the type with the large gas balloon on the roof? The charcoal vans were great for a heat in the winter days, or lighting your cigarette to save a match.

Many old family firms which were household names to Dubliners have gone, while quite a few old names are still with us, although in many cases only the name is there, and the old business is now part of a large group. Pidgeons, Steins, Stumps, Youkstetters and May Clarke were best for sausages, black and white pudding and pigs' feet. Hafners made quality sausages for years but they were taken over a few years ago by H. Williams. Once you could go to Ruddles, Taylors and Lundy Foot of Parliament Street for your snuff. Other Dublin companies of renown were Kelly's Cigars in Camden Street, The Irish Tobacco Company on Merchant's Quay and The Dublin Japan Works in Jervis Street — they were expert Japanners, Enamellers and Platers. Devlin's of Francis Street made clay pipes. You can still go to Barnardo's of Grafton Street, established 1819, for your fur coat, and to Parkes of the Coombe for hardware. Parkes are an old trading house who made many Dublin firms' trading tokens. West's of Grafton Street have for generations produced beautiful, expertly designed and expensive jewellery. Thomas Mason traded for many years in Palace Street, just beside The Castle, until a disastrous fire gutted the premises. The building is still there, just as the fire brigade left it, but the business continues at 5 Crane Lane nearby. Mason's built up over the years a big collection of photographic plates, and many of these were lost in the fire.

Thomas Read of 4 Parliament Street was established in 1670, and are one of the oldest cutlers in the world. They have a knife which has five-hundred-and-seventy-six different blades on it. They also have the Lilliputian Scissors, which measures a quarter of an inch. Read's originally started business at The Blind Quay near Fishamble Street, but later moved to Crane Lane, which incidentally, gets its name from the crane that unloaded goods at the Quays opposite the lane, and not from a bird. They remained in Crane Lane until the Wide Streets Commissioners laid out Parliament Street, and then moved their shop to its present location. They still retain a workshop in Crane Lane where knives, scissors and all kinds of implements are repaired and sharpened.

The interior of the shop is full of atmosphere, a real throwback to times gone by. Many of the display cases, drawers and counters are from the original shop. Read's also made swords and surgical instruments, and in the days when the surgeons from the College in Stephen's Green were breaking new ground in their profession, Read's got the job of making and designing the instruments from the surgeon's rough sketches.

The interior of Read's Cutlery Shop showing some of the original sword cases.

Left – the Daisy Market which is off Capel Street and right a versatile businessman of 1917.

Carton is another old name still with us. You go to Carton Bros. of Halston Street for eggs, butter, cheese, poultry, game, and to E. & D. Carton of Smithfield for corn, hay, potatoes, seed, grain etc. Dublin's Cattle Market was at one time held in Smithfield and this accounts for many of the old merchants still to be found in the Square. The courtyard of Carton's has a real old world feel about it. It is not unusual even today to find a horse-and-cart arriving to collect fodder and other supplies. C. Dodd and Sons are another old firm in the same business, and across the cobbled square is Jameson's Distillery, now alas disused.

The Dame Street and College Green area has for many years been insurance land. "The Sun" claim to be the oldest insurance company in the world and were founded in 1710, but the Commercial Union claims foundation in 1696. The fire brigade service was once run by the insurance companies but they only threw water and sand on the houses that were insured, and many a merchant regretted the day he forgot to pay his premium. Before this the parish churches organised the pumps, buckets and ladders, and each parish acted as its own fire-service. Today's Dublin Fire Brigade is a descendant of the service run by the insurance companies.

Yes, we had umbrella merchants, clock merchants, but what about a gas merchant? "You're a gas merchant", meant that you were terribly funny. The dentist was the first gas merchant, who, to stop you roaring with pain, gave you laughing gas so that you laughed with pain instead, and the dentist became known as the gas merchant among other names. I remember one time saying to a person, "yer man is a gas merchant". "No he's not", said my friend, "he works in the Corporation".

Markets, markets, markets. Here are a few names once familiar to Dubliners. The Camden, The Castle, Masons, The Food, Potato, Fruit. There was also the Leinster Market, pushed out of the way to make room for the Gas Company in D'Olier Street. The Bird Market in Dublin has a long history. It moved from time to time around the Liberties of Dublin. For a long time it stood in Bride Street at the rere of St. Patrick's Cathedral, opposite Wood Street. Many a child went home from the Bird Market carrying a white paper bag thinking it contained a bird. 'Mister, Mister, give us a bird, give us a bird Mister'. To get rid of the non-buying children, the dealers would stick their hand into a paper bag, twist the top of it and say 'There now and don't open the bag until you get home'. On the child's return journey to the market the dealer would convince him that it must have flown out of the bag. 'Go away out of that' he would say, 'you lost the bloody one I gave you last week. Go down to the Cats and Dogs Home and get yourself a wow-wow'.

"Two shillings each the yellow canaries. How about a nice budgie? I'll have eagles next" ... The Bird Market goes back hundreds of years and was always very popular with Dublin people. In the early days the birds were sold by sailors who came into Dublin on foreign ships. At one time the bird was carried home in your pocket or hands. Later still it was in brown or white paper bags, or black sugar bags.

The glamour of the Markets remains — in fact Dublin is again becoming a City of Markets. Its a far cry from The Daisy to the Dandelion, or from the Iveagh to The Liberty. Moore Street, Thomas Street, Henry Street, Francis Street, Liffey Street at Christmas time all have markets big and small. Hector

Grey still sells at the Ha'penny Bridge. The Balloon Man, the tin whistles 10 pence each, or 'the last of the Long Decorations' are familiar to the real Dubliner.

You can buy a bronze bracelet, prints of Dublin, books by the dozen, a bed chamber pot, a hall table, an umbrella, shoes for every shape and size of foot, Long Johns or Jockey Briefs, Hot Pants, Mini Skirts, Maxi Dresses and Leather Skirts, Drawers, Belts, Bags and Boots.

Any day of the week you will find the streets around the Fruit and Vegetable Market off Capel Street, blocked with orange boxes, crates of apples, bananas and forklift trucks. Nearby a man in huge rubber boots and a long apron is hosing down the floor of the Fish Market. Both markets are run by the Corporation and traders rent stalls to sell and auction their produce.

Nearby, in East Arran Street old ladies rummage through huge piles of jackets, coats, frocks and shoes. This is where you will find the Daisy Market. It dates back a long way and some of the women have been selling here for fifty years.

Just off Moore Street the last tattered remains of The Anglesea Markets can be seen. Business is still going on, but the lot will soon come crumbling down when the Corporation press ahead with their new plans for this area.

The Cattle Market between Prussia Street and the North Circular Road is now quiet — but it was not long ago that cattle were driven through these streets, and small boys with big sticks beat the poor beasts on their way to the Dublin Cattle Market.

So get up on your bike and do a tour of Dublin Markets, and you are bound to come home with a bargain or two.

A notice still in place near Mountjoy Jail dating from the days when cattle were driven up these streets to and from the market between Prussia Street and North Circular Road.

A Trip Down the Port

Every now and then, a few men dressed in bright yellow oilskin coats and hats stand on O'Connell Bridge collecting funds for the Royal National Life-Boat Institution. You can put your donation into a boat-shaped box or into a pipeline running from the bridge to a lifeboat, gaily decorated with flags and bunting in the River Liffey. These are the men that go down to the sea, risking their lives to save others in distress in heavy seas off the port of Dublin.

Look! they are moving off, let's go with them and explore the port. We're moving now in the ripples of the Helga Gunboat which travelled these waters in 1916 to shell Liberty Hall and Dublin City. On your right is Aston's Quay, the Scotch House and Hawkins Street, named after a man who planned the Hawkins Wall to push back the river Liffey and reclaim the land at Burgh Quay. Next the Corn Exchange and the Conciliation Hall used by the Young Irelanders and the Repeal Association. The Irish Press where Padraig Pearse's mother started the printing machine to produce the first issue in 1931. The

From the Illustrated London News of 1846 this view shows the port, the Custom House and Amiens Street Railway Station. The Loop Line Bridge was not built at that time.

Dublin's glory, James Gandon's Custom House viewed from the other side of the Liffey.

name 'Irish Press' came from J. J. McGarrity's old newspaper in Philadelphia. Liberty Hall, the home of Larkin, Connolly. Mallin and Partridge — soars sky-wards; it was originally the Northumberland Hotel. Liberty Hall was the first trade union headquarters in Dublin — the sign over the door read: "We serve neither King nor Kaiser but Ireland" and the Irish Citizen Army in their green and grey uniforms together with their Chief of Staff, Michael Mallin, spent time practising foot and arms drill in Beresford Place. Willie Oman, the bugler, has just sounded the fall-in. Pearse has arrived with the boys of *Scoil Eanna* and that is James Connolly standing on the steps. Now we pass under two bridges, Butt Bridge on the River Liffey and the Loop Line Railway Bridge over the Liffey. Isaac Butt, the Fenians' friend who took their brief in Green Street Courthouse became a pauper, locked in the debtor's prison without a friend, and died in loneliness.

Dublin's glory, Dublin's pride and joy, James Gandon's Custom House — a stone of beauty, its green dome, its clock, its long room, its steps and its gardens. Look back and have a clear view, Dubliners can't see it from the other side of the bridge, the Loopline should never have been built. The stone carvings were designed by Edward Smyth. There are fourteen beautiful key-stones, one for Anna Livia, one for the Atlantic Ocean and twelve for the princi-pal rivers in Ireland. Its the finest Custom House in the world. John Beresford laid the foundation stone and the building was opened in 1791. The architect, James Gandon, born in England, was the grandson of a Huguenot who fled from France on the Revocation of the Edict of Nantes. During the Black & Tan days, the Dublin I.R.A. burned the Custom House which contained huge numbers of records of the British Administration system. It has been said that this action by the I.R.A. was one of the factors which led to the truce of July, 1921.

This port dates back to the Bronze Age when Dubliners sailed from here to the seven seas — our exports were gold and copper from the Wicklow

Mines. Trade and shipping became so heavy over the years that the larger boats could only come as far as the Pool of Clontarf, and others had to land at Dalkey and Dun Laoghaire (Kingstown). Improvements were made in the 13th century but still the port couldn't cope with all the ships. As each decade went by more improvements were carried out, and in 1649, Oliver Cromwell landed his ships and 13,000 soldiers at Ringsend.

The merchants of Dublin still pressed the Dublin Corporation for more developments, and for the clearing of the port of ballast dumped by incoming ships. The Corporation wouldn't spend the few shillings so the merchants petitioned Queen Anne and bribed her husband with a hundred yards of best Holland Duck Sail Cloth. Yer man took the bribe. The Queen passed the Act and the Dublin Corporation had to set up a special committee to look after the port and ballast.

The year 1707 was the start of a great era for the port – the new South Wall and later the North Wall were planned. The Bull Wall, designed by the port's own engineer, George Halpin, was added in 1820. Captain Blyth *(The Bounty)* paid a visit to advise on development matters, and also the Poolbeg Lighthouse. The idea of the Bull Wall was to quicken the speed of the ebbing tide, free the bay of obstacles and give greater force to the waters into the port. The Bull Wall gave us the Bull Island where we have, today, one of the world's finest and most important wildlife breeding grounds – a bird sanctuary in a capital city with the greatest collection in numbers and types of wild fowl. For students who are studying nature and wildlife, this is a Paradise.

There is the 100 ton crane which was brought into the port nearly 70 years ago, where we can also see Misery Hill where the old lepers lived, and where the City Sheriff had his hanging-ground. The road beyond leads to Raytown (Ringsend) and the old Pidgeon House, named after John Pidgeon who was caretaker of tools and equipment at the building of the South Wall. The Pidgeon House later became a musical Tavern, a Military Post and now it is an E.S.B. generating station.

There was a time around 1936 when you could take a trip around the port and bay of Dublin in the Royal Iris for a half-a-crown.

Hidden Places

Around St Marys Abbey

Now it was like this. On a warm sunny September afternoon in the 11th century, Clunlif and his wife Dervogil were sitting outside their house and vast lands on the northern banks of the River Liffey. Clunlif Gill Moholomoc was one of the high-ranking chiefs of Dublin and was the owner of a fair bit of property inside the walls of Dublin City. Clunlif was stone blind as was his closest kinsman Malachi. I suppose this was the reason he chose to live beyond the walls and waters of Dublin.

Well himself and the wife were enjoying the sunshine and at the same time giving alms to the poor who were always welcome. Suddenly, Clunlif, who was sitting on the log of a tree got the sweet smell of the apple blossom. He put his hand along the tree log, felt an apple, plucked it and bit hard into its juicy centre. His eyes opened and for the first time in many years he could see the Danish Fort, the Liffey Waters, his kinsmen, his wife and his lands. He then saw two more apples on the log. He called his wife and Malachi. They both ate of the fruit and Malachi's sight was restored. The miracle would not be forgotten, for Clunlif was a holy, generous man. Soon the trio, Clunlif, Dervogil and Malachi decided to erect an Abbey which they would dedicate to Mary, the mother of God. The Abbey was handed over to the followers of St. Benedict known as The Black Monks.

In 1139, The Benedictines adopted the Cistercian Rule and got the full approval and blessing of Pope Eugenius III. The Abbey of St. Mary claimed all the lands north of the Liffey from their Abbey House which stood near Ormond Quay to the lands of Clunlif (Clonliffe), Drumcondra, beside the Tolka River. In the other direction they claimed the fields of Oxmantown to Salock Woods at the Phoenix Park swinging gates. The Abbot and his Monks became very rich and influential. They had their own fleet of vessels and their own herring sheds and claimed not only taxes on the fish from the Liffey, but everything that sank or was shipwrecked on the Liffey bed.

They had the best of both worlds and got a Liberty from King Henry II and another Liberty from the Pope in Rome. Henry's Charter confirmed all their claims to land and property within and without the walls of Dublin City. King John, who followed Henry in the 13th century, gave several Charters to the Abbey and placed them under his direct care. They were also under the direct care of Rome. The wealth and influence of the Abbey increased and the Abbot sat in Parliament as a spiritual Lord with a temporal eye. The Abbot

On the left is the small door in Meetinghouse Lane which leads to the Chapter House of St. Mary's Abbey and above an old drawing of Silken Thomas in the Council Chamber (Chapter House).

soon adopted the same customs as the Abbot of the Liberty of St. Thomas Court and Donore. He had his Abbey Church, his Palace, his Dungeons and his Gallows and sat at times as a Lord Chief Justice.

Down the years some of the Abbots considered themselves more powerful than the English King or the Roman Pope. When the Prior and Canons of Christchurch Cathedral tried to cut in on the Abbot's treasure (1214) they were opposed with words and swords. Christchurch backed down, but it was decreed to excommunicate the Abbot and Monks of St. Mary's Abbey. One year later Felix O'Ruadan, Archbishop of Tuam came to St. Mary's Abbey and stated that he had resigned and wished to spend the rest of his days as a simple Monk. The graves of Felix, Clunlif, Dervogil and Malachi and the Monks and Abbots that died before the suppression lie under the roadway of Capel Street and Mary's Abbey.

The only remaining relics today are the lands of Clonliffe (Holy Cross College) and the Chapter House in Meetinghouse Lane off Mary's Abbey. The key to the Chapter House can be had at Number 9. Ask for Mrs. Brennan, and the good woman herself will show you the Council Chamber where Silken Thomas threw down the Sword of State in 1534 and went into rebellion against the English Crown. Silken's father was The Earl of Kildare, Lord Deputy of Ireland. The Earl had been summoned to London and a rumour reached Silken that his father had been murdered in the Tower of London.

'Silken' (so called because of his fancy clothes) marched into the Council Chamber and instead of taking his father's place at the head of the

Newgate Jail which adjoined Green Street Courthouse.

Council Table, he began to curse the King of England. The wise Lords tried to quieten his voice, "keep calm" they said, "wait for more news, send a messenger, wait, don't rush". Silken was about to sit down when one of his followers plucked the strings of a Geraldine War Harp with the Earl's battle tune. The war music boiled the blood of Silken Thomas and down went the sword. "To hell with the King" he said and stormed from the Chamber to head an attack on the Castle and Dublin City. Silken failed. He was invited to London for peace talks, and as soon as he and his five uncles arrived they were put in chains and later hanged at Tyburn Cross.

The statue of Our Lady of Dublin in Whitefriar Street Church (Aungier Street) is another true relic of St. Mary's Abbey. This statue, carved in wood, had a strange history and for several hundred years was used as a pigs' water trough in East Arran Street. In 1824 Rev. John Spratt, Prior of the Carmelite Order, discovered and purchased it in a second-hand junk shop in Capel Street. East Arran Street was originally Boot Lane with its several alleys and rows of unusual names, Manypenny Yard, Brush Row, Lucky Hall, Petticoat Lane, all leading to Green Street Courthouse, the "new" Newgate Jail, George's Hill and Cuckoo Lane.

Today a handball alley, a children's playground, a few seats for old men and women and a memorial statue mark the site of the jail (demolished 1893). It was here that Lord Edward Fitzgerald died in his prison cell, the Shears brothers John and Henry stood side-by-side waiting on the hangmans axe outside the Newgate door.

Green Street Courthouse, which is still in use today, has been the place of trial for Republicans and separatists since 1796. The first Belfast Republican to enter its door was John Robb, printer of *The Northern Star,* the official organ of The United Irishmen's Society. In September 1796 Robb, Samuel Neilson (the Editor) and Thomas Russell arrived. They had been arrested on a sedition charge. They were taken from their homes in Belfast and driven by horse cart, day and night, non-stop, to Newgate Jail.

In 1970, a descendant of John Robb, bearing the same name, and noted as one of the North's most respected moderates, showed me and others in The Tailors' Hall, Back Lane, a number of letters and keepsakes dating back to 1796. Under the Courthouse are the same cells used by Emmet , his men and the men of 1798, John Mitchell and Young Irelanders Rossa, and the Fenians — Brady, Curley, Kelly, Cafferty, Fagan, Skin the Goat and the Irish National Invincibles also spent time here.

In the year 1815 the last public whipping took place from the gates of Green Street Courthouse to City Hall (Royal Exchange) on Cork Hill. The victim was William Horish, "The Master Sweep" who lived in Dame Court. This was by no means the first whipping that William Horish had received. In July 1803, he was arrested on the word of an informer named Carroll, and he was taken to Tyrone House. This large stone building in Marlborough Street known as Beresford's Riding House Establishment, was used as a torture and flogging house in 1798 and 1803. It appears that Major Sirr failed to break the spirit of William Horish and continued to harrass and torture him on trumped-up charges, even twelve years after Emmet 's Rising.

Before we leave this haunted centre of Dublin, spare a thought for the scores who went to their deaths and left their last letters written to wives, children, fathers, mothers and other relations, in the hands of Major Sirr. He never delivered the letters, but kept them in his own private papers. Their letters are now in the Archives of Trinity College.

Beyond Green Street lies "George's Hill", the convent school of Teresa Mullally, Nano Nagle and the Presentation Sisters. Teresa was born in Pill Lane (Chancery Street) in 1728. Her ambition in life was to found a school and teach children. Despite Castle spies and priest-hunters, she rented, at her own expense, a house in Mary's Lane, and from a small class of 12 children, she built up several other classes until she decided she needed a larger building to cater for her pupils. In 1787 she moved her school to the old glass works on George's Hill. A friendship with a girl named Nano Nagle led to the introduction of The Presentation Nuns to George's Hill.

After the suppression of St. Mary's Abbey around 1539, the lands became the property of King Henry VIII. The next owner was a man named John Piphoe, a son of Adam Piphoe (Clontarf Castle). When Piphoe died, the lands were claimed by his widow. However Dublin Castle had other ideas and tried to take the land from Mrs. Piphoe. After enquiries it was found that the old lady was 98 years old and very frail. "Ah leave it with her" they said, "Sure she will be dead in a few weeks". Dead, how are you! She lived another twenty years and saw many of the Castle grabbers under the clay before she finally died at the age of 118 years. Her grave is in the vaults of St. Michan's Church. She died in 1669.

Jervis Street gets its name from the next owner of the lands of St. Mary's Abbey. Sir Humphrey Jervis, Lord Mayor of Dublin, built a bridge across the Liffey facing Dublin Castle, and also laid out Capel Street and the adjoining streets. He gave the first honours in names to the Viceroy who in 1678 was Arthur Capel, Earl of Essex. So we have Capel Street, Essex Street, Essex Quay and Essex Bridge. The street with his own name "Jervis" has the distinction of Dublin's first and oldest hospital. The old Charitable Infirmary Jervis Street Hospital dates from 1718. One of the wards faces the spot where Wolfe Tone was born in June 1763 (Stafford Street, now Wolfe Tone Street). Another ward overlooks St. Mary's Church and graveyard.

This church is steeped in history and was one of the first churches in Dublin to display by notice-board its historic traditions and connections with Dublin and Ireland's history. The church dates back to the year 1691, and was the baptismal church of Tone and Sean O'Casey. The park beside the church is well laid out and contains a memorial stone to Wolfe Tone.

The next time you're coming down Capel Street think of Number 27 (the street has since been re-numbered) and try and imagine poor King James II making coins from tin cans, pots and pans, cannon gun and cannon balls. *Yes,* this was James's Mint House, but after the Battle of the Boyne, King Billy came down Capel Street and kicked the tin cans all around St. Mary's Abbey. Did you ever play "Kick the Can" when you were a child? All you want is a tin can and a good pair of hobnail boots with iron tips on the toes and heels.

James minted nearly a million pounds between 18th June 1689 and 15th June 1690. Money valued by James at £21,886 was only worth £642 in real terms. Ah its a pity you're dead James! You died too soon. Sure in 1972 I saw an advert in *Irish Numismatics,* the coin magazine, which stated "For sale James II Gunmoney Crown struck in gold £5000".

Old St. Mary's Church from Wolfe Tone Street.

Well thank you Sir Humphrey Jervis. You didn't do a bad job. Fair play to ya... and your street "Jervis" also has another proud distinction. It provided a birthplace for Dublin's greatest historian, Sir John T. Gilbert, author of three volumes on the History of the old City and Southside of Dublin. His attention to detail in the Calendar of Ancient Records of Dublin is monumental. Volume after volume he produced, and recorded The White Book, The Blue Book, The Chain Book, The City Clock which the Corpo was going to give to Oxmantown because the fellows in Thomas Street would not wind it every day. Ah Gilbert — they say he never wrote a word about the north side or the place of his birth — sometimes we are inclined to forget his *Charularies of St. Mary's Abbey.*

If you can find the time, take a trip down the steps to the stone Chapter House. When you step onto the stone floor about eight feet down, you are at the original street level of Dublin town eight hundred years ago. If ever the houses and buildings around this area are knocked down, the National Museum should move in, for under the ground is the buried treasure of Dublin's history and its great abbey.

King James II.ᵈ Mint Houfe, Nº. 27, Capel St.
Where the late Thomas Sheridan was born.

The Five Lamps

The five lamps stand on a concrete island at the junction of five roads. Let's make five short tours – all within five minutes from the five lamps –

1. Across the road is Aldborough House with memories of Edward Stratford, Viscount Amiens, Earl of Aldborough. He had the house built in 1796 and it cost £40,000. It was another Georgian beauty and the last of the great town houses of the period, but the wife didn't like it. She said it was too damp and too near Mud Island, so back she went to Stratford-on-Avon. However they came back again to build the town of Stratford-on-Slaney, in Wicklow. Edward even had a theatre in Aldborough House but it was a bit of a flop.

The house was then rented by Von-Feinagle for his Feinaglian School. He named the school "Luxembourg College" and had a system of education on the exercise of the memory – no blackboards, chalk or writing books, just a Memory College with every subject learned at the finger-tips. He turned "scholars" out the gate in their dozens. He died in 1819 and the house became vacant for a few years. The Red-Coat soldiers used it as a temporary barracks, and in 1843, when Dan O'Connell organised his Clontarf meeting, the barracks was filled with 3,000 troops. Dan called off the meeting and sent special messengers to notify several people in person – the messengers conveyed the sad news to the people who had marched from Wexford, and they just hung about in groups under the eyes of the Red-Coats beside the Five Lamps.

2. Running between Summerhill and Amiens Street is Buckingham Street – no, its not called after the Palace, but after the Viceroy, the Marquess of Buckingham. Did you know that one of the Buckinghams gave us the first mini-skirt? Well it happened like this – the King of England always washed his hands after a day's hunting and Buckingham's job was to hold the bucket of water. This day as he was holding the bucket, didn't Cardinal Wolsey come in before the King; 'oh good', he said and dipped his dirty maulers into the bucket of water. Buckingham was furious, so he threw the bucket, water and all, over Wolsey. "I'll get you Buckingham" he said, "tomorrow in the House of Lords I'll tread on the tail of your coat". The next day Buckingham appeared wearing only a leather jerkin (mini-skirt size!). "You won't get a chance to tread on my coat tails", said Buckingham, "this is the length of my coat from now on".

Number 36 Buckingham Street was the home of John O'Donovan, the father of a family of Fenians; one of his sons, also named John, manufactured rifles and bullets in this house. Rossa, Stephens, Thomas Clarke and Luby held Council meetings in the front parlour. Across the road, where the pawn office is today, was the local Royal Irish Constabulary barracks. Little did the 'polis'

The Five Lamps with Aldborough House behind. Five streets meet here, Amiens Street, North Strand Road, Portland Row, Seville Place and Killarney Street. A storm whipped one of the lamps away shortly after the drawing was done and it has not re-appeared to date.

know that a Fenian Headquarters was right opposite their hall-door. John O'Donovan was a great scholar and translated many Gaelic Manuscripts including the works of the Four Masters in 1864. Because of his great learning he had many academic friends, including the Provost and several Fellows of Trinity College Dublin. The ancient Annals of the Kingdom of Ireland and the Martyrology of Donegal, a calendar of the Saints of Ireland, written by the Four Masters in 1630, lay in dust for 234 years until they were transcribed by O'Curry and translated by John O'Donovan in Buckingham Street Dublin.

At the top of the hill, turn to the right, look into the Town of the Poor — "Ballybough" noted today for racing pigeons and luxury pigeon lofts. Go around to the right again and into Portland Row and down the hill back to the Five Lamps.

3. Do you see the Railway Bridge? Well, if you don't, walk once around the Five Lamps and you're sure to spot it. What did you say? You saw two, well I need only one for my story or the Five Lamps, Five Tours, Five Minutes will lose its appeal. 555 State Express cigarettes, during the last war, were a God-send to smokeless Dublin. They also manufactured State Express 333 and the little shop at the corner had buckets of them.

Look down Seville Place, better still walk down to the bridge, and notice St. Laurence O'Toole's Church standing in the distance. The Pagan O'Leary helped build that one too and Joe Clarke went to school beside it. The master used to mark his boots with white chalk when he missed his lessons. But even then Joe was a rebel, he used to rub out the chalk marks and the master could never remember whether he had marked them or not. Every Monday morning, our laundry van passed down Seville Place, I always had a good look at the Church and the iron gate at the end of Guild Street. The gate seemed to draw me and I often wondered what it was about it that compelled me to look at it. Fourteen years later I was the Manager of a coal yard behind that iron gate in Guild Street. Across the road from it was Synott's shop and in Black and Tan days the iron gate led into an I.R.A. arms dump.

Gild Street leads to Dublin dockland with Spencer Dock on the waterfront. This is another world, another city with talk of fillers, breasters, casuals and button men, screening, tapping out, lower your gib, singer-outs and hooker-ons. At one time it was no work in the rain, no money to spare, just 'under the hammer' and the £5 kick at Christmas which was paid back by the week. Beero hour, the Jade, the Myrtle, or Polish coal which was called continental — for fear of religious reaction. I know what you're thinking, this is a hairy five minutes' walk from the Five Lamps, so I'd better stop or next I'll have you in the ferry crossing the river to the great South Wall. The bridge at Seville Place was where Joe Poole shot the Informer. Joe was an Invincible and was later hanged in Richmond Jail. The story of Pat O'Donnell and James Carey is well known but little is known today of Joseph Poole who shot the first informer under the bridge down the street from the Five Lamps.

4. Now don't tell me its more than five minutes' walk to Gloucester Street — well even if its ten, its worth going there. The Street, The Diamond, The Place and Kane's Court. This is really Kane country. The Duke of Gloucester was only the son of a King, but Robert Kane was the son of a Dublin scientist. He was born in Gloucester Street on 24th September 1809. At an early age he showed great interest in his father's work, chemistry. The father taught the son well, and young Robert entered the Meath Hospital as a medical student. Before he was 21 years old he was Professor of Chemistry in the Apothecaries Hall, a position he held for fourteen years. He published several books and founded the Dublin Journal of Medical Science. Kane's works, his life, his teaching and industrial ideas would fill many volumes.

He loved Dublin and Ireland and was in a sense the first Sinn Feiner (Ourselves Alone). He made proposals for water power at Shannon and also peat power. He made proposals concerning glass, sand, gypsum and the urgent need for agricultural education. If they had listened to Kane, acted as Kane advised, the Famine might never have happened. Go into the National Library and get the books of Robert Kane and discover the mind of this great man who was born in Dublin down the street from the Five Lamps.

A turn off the street where Kane was born brings you into Cumberland Street, the birthplace of Sir Charles Cameron, the greatest Medical Health Officer that Dublin City ever had. — the man who saved the lives of thousands of Dubliners and who rid Dublin of its fever epidemics. He was head of the Freemason Order, yet spent his life working for the poor of Dublin who were 95% Catholic. He was a legend in his lifetime and I wonder what he would say today if he could see the poor of Dublin buying second-hand clothes from the gutters in the street where he was born.

5. The bridge at The Royal Canal at North Strand Road is the spot where Matt Talbot decided to give up the drink and lead his holy life. The bridge is named Newcomen after a director of The Royal Canal. Beyond the bridge lies Bessborough Avenue, which brings to mind Dublin's Association with two ladies and blue stockings — Lady Eleanor Butler of Kilkenny Castle and her friend, Sarah Ponsonby, who came from the family of the Earls of Bessborough, who ran away together and settled down in a house in the vale of Llangollen. For over 70 years they were known as the Ladies of Llangollen and were often visited by many Earls and Lords of Ireland and England. They lived contented lives among their books and gardens and knitted blue stockings. They were both 90 years of age when they died, Lady Butler 1829 and Miss Ponsonby 1831. I visited their home which, today, is a tourist attraction. It is in a beautiful vale, miles from nowhere and I could almost see them sitting in their garden drinking tea which had just been served by their Irish maid, Mary Carroll. Its a far cry from Llangollen, Wales to the North Strand Dublin, but then many names in Dublin have a cry to the end of the earth.

The Five Lamps were erected as a memorial to General Henry Hall, a native of Galway who served in the Indian Army. The Five Lamps have links with the Punjab, Aliwal, and other Indian battles where Irishmen fell in their thousands. 90% of the British Indian Army were recruited during the famine days when the choice for many was starve to death or see glory, the world, have Indian servants, a horse, a sword, a smart uniform and full rations and beer daily. Pay was seven shillings a week, which was worth a fortune in India.

An advertisement of 1816 for the Feinagle School at Aldborough House (see page 104).

SCHOOLS.

FEINAIGLIAN INSTITUTION.

THE Committee, anxious that the operation of the System of Instruction introduced into this Country by Professor Von Feinaigle, should be subjected to the severest test of public opinion, have uniformly given to the half-yearly Examinations all possible publicity. To extend the opportunities of forming a correct judgment on a subject so interesting to the community, the late Examinations were continued during four successive days, in presence of many individuals the most eminently qualified to appreciate the effects of that system, in the progressive improvement of the Pupils of the Institution. To the unbiased opinion of judges so competent, the Committee most willingly submit the decision of the questions, how far the knowledge acquired by the Pupils may be considered sound and radical, and how far the practical results of two years' application of the Professor's system, are decisive of its superiority over all the modes of instruction hitherto employed in Public Seminaries. Of that decision, though formed by persons as yet necessarily unacquainted with the nature and principles of the system itself, the Committee entertain no apprehension, but confidently rest upon it the character of the Institution.

ADJUDICATION OF PREMIUMS.

After this last Examination, the places of merit and distinction, as Decurios of their respective Classes, were adjudged to Masters Semple, Murton, M'Auley, Henry (Thomas,) and Knox (Thomas;) and as first Comites, to Masters Belcher (Arth.) Welsh, Lloyd, Webber, and Crampton. Premiums were also adjudged, and on the 23d. were publicly conferred on the following young Gentlemen:—

IN THE SIXTH OR SENIOR CLASS.

For best answering in *Greek, Latin, French, History, Geography, Mathematics,* and *Natural History*—To Master Semple.
In *Greek, Latin, Mathematics, History,* and *Geography*—To Masters Belcher (Arth.) and Hodson.
In *French and Mathematics*—To Master Winter.

In *Greek and Mathematics*—To Master Dwyer.
In *French and Geography*—To Master M'Kane.
In *Latin*—To Master Ferguson.
And in *History*—To Master Robert Jones.

IN THE FIFTH CLASS.

For best answering in *Greek, Latin, History,* and *Geography*—To Masters Murton and Welsh; and after them to Masters Mahon, Goold and Warham.
In *Greek and Latin*—To Master Molloy.
In *Greek and History*—To Master John Stafford.
In *Greek and Geography*—To Master Synnott.
In *Greek*—To Master Graves.
In this Class, general Premiums were adjudged to Masters Bourne, Smyly (Cecil,) Allen, Knox (Edmond,) and White (Thomas,) for diligence, good conduct, and relative good progress.

IN THE FOURTH CLASS.

For best answering in *Greek, Latin,* and *History*—To Masters M'Auley, Lloyd and Baker.
In *Greek and Latin*—To Masters Belcher (Thomas), and Bride.
In *Greek*—To Masters Guy Atkinson, Edward Singleton, Thos. M'Cheane, and Wm. Singleton.
To Master George Atkinson a General Premium was adjudged.

IN THE THIRD CLASS.

For best answering in *Latin, English,* and *History*—To Masters Henry (Thomas) and Webber.
In *Latin and English*—To Masters Smyly (Josiah), Ryall (Phineas), Leader and Gamble.
In *Latin*—To Masters M'Alpine (Wm.) and Hayes.
To Masters Clanchy, Murray (Edward), and M'Alpine (Irwin), General Premiums were adjudged.

IN THE SECOND CLASS.

For best answering in *Latin and English*—To Masters Knox (Thomas), Crampton and D'Arcy.
In *Latin*—To Masters Creagh, Andrews (John), Maxwell, and Ryall (Wm.)
To Masters Crowe, Magrath, and Davis (Wm.), General Premiums were adjudged.

The Royal Circus

I'm sitting in the middle of The Royal Circus as I write these words, but its not exactly the type of private mansion Luke Gardiner had in mind as part of his grand design. The 1798 rebellion changed many things. It also killed Luke Gardiner at the battle of New Ross, and deprived Dublin of its Royal Circus.

Mountjoy Jail was built on Famine Relief Work and its door was opened for guests in 1860 and it's still in business today. I have examined in detail for several hours its structure, its wall-thickness, the strength of its grill-type iron-barred windows and you can take my word for it, its a very solid structure, good for at least another hundred years. The builders of Mountjoy Jail did a bloody fine job for a few bowls of soup. I would hate to think what they would have built if they had been paid wages.

The reason the jail was built was because the people of Botany Bay complained to the King of England about all the convicts being dumped outside their hall-doors. O'Donovan Rossa, Manager of *The Irish People,* the Fenian newspaper, spent Christmas of 1865 inside Mountjoy Jail. Everyday I walk in Rossa's footsteps around the exercise yard, or look out into the wood yard where Thomas Ashe chopped wood for the jail boilers. The place is haunted with memories. (I nearly spent Christmas of 1973 here but like many others was whisked away to Portlaoise following a surprise helicopter escape). I cannot help wondering how many more editors of *An Phoblacht* will spend time here

Fifteen paces from my cell leads to the hang-house door. There are times when I can almost see Kevin Barry, head erect, walking past me to meet his God. The story of the jail would fill many books and perhaps someday a pen will scribe words into a volume named "Mountjoy Jail Journal".

Luke Gardiner, Lord Mountjoy, was the largest land-owner on the northside of Dublin City. He was the man whose family built Sackville Street, Mountjoy Square, and the other North Dublin Georgian Avenues, and he had plans to build a Royal Circus where the Mater Hospital and Mountjoy Jail stand today. The Royal Circus was to consist of several splendid private Georgian mansions, miniatures of Castletown House Celbridge, with twelve grand avenues leading into the Circus. It was to be a question of, the richer you are the nearer you live to The Royal Circus, and those in the Circus itself were to have been the elite of the elite.

The plans were drawn up, and the first avenue was actually laid out. The Gardens of Mount Eccles House, the residence of Sir John Eccles, Lord Mayor of Dublin in 1710, provided the site for the first avenue. This was Eccles Street. Synott Place, Cowley Place and Elizabeth Street were decided on as three other avenues. However, the 1798 Rebellion was erupting and Luke Gardiner cast aside his Royal Circus plans and rode to Wexford at the head of the Dublin Militia. That was the last time Luke saw Dublin — he was killed in action. After his death, work on the Royal Circus stopped and Luke's plans were never completed.

Across the road from the Mater Hospital (1861) in Eccles Street stands a Celtic Cross, a monument to the Four Masters. Why it was erected here is a mystery — the Franciscans asked for it to be erected beside their friary on Merchant's Quay, but their wish was not granted. The monument is almost hidden behind railings at the corner of Eccles Street and Berkeley Road. The inscription is in Irish, English and Latin.

The annals of the kingdom of Ireland are known as the annals of The Four Masters. The contents of the annals took more than ten years to gather. Moore in his history of Ireland says: "The precision with which the Irish Annalists have recorded month, day, hour of an eclipse of the sun in the year 664 affords an instance of the exceeding accuracy with which they observed and noted passing events". Dublin is mentioned more than 250 times in the annals of the Four Masters, which were completed in 1637. Some of the recording was carried out in Dublin.

Dublin had neglected the Four Masters until Sir Robert William Wilde suggested in 'The Nation' newspaper of November 1871 that a memorial be erected. Sir William was dead before the task was completed in 1876. We can be very certain that Sir William Wilde never intended his dream to be hidden in a spot where it is unnoticed by the thousands who visit the Mater Hospital.

If you walk slowly down Eccles Street you might meet Joyce's Leopold Bloom who lived in Number Seven, or Brendan Behan's "Hostage" being taken into a house in Nelson Street. If you see the sheriff on his horse outside Number 64 Eccles Street he's waiting to take Isaac Butt, the home rule leader, to the Debtors Prison. Francis Johnston, the architect of St. George's Church, lived in the same house years before.

Luke Gardiner would get quite a shock if he came back to see his grand square today. The propped-up house is No. 50 Mountjoy Square and is owned by the Irish Georgian Society.

Francis Johnston was born in Armagh in 1760, and came to Dublin when he was a teenager. He was taught by Thomas Cooley, the man who designed the Royal Exchange (City Hall). Johnston designed many other fine buildings including the G.P.O. in O'Connell Street (1814). His masterpiece is St. George's Church in Hardwicke Street which dates from 1802 and cost almost £90,000 to build. It stands 200 ft. high with a five storey clock tower and spire over its roof, which can be seen all over Dublin. St. George's is a beautiful church and well worth a visit. The Iron Duke, Sir Arthur Wellesley K.B., Duke of Wellington, married Catherine Sarah Dorothea Packenham in St. George's on 10th April, 1806.

In 1823 Francis Johnston took the eight bells (which he used to chime regularly to the annoyance of his neighbours) from his back garden and presented them to St. George's Church. He was just in time, because the first peal of the muffled bells in St. George's was for his own funeral.

Beside the church in Temple Street is the Children's Hospital, and Number 14 in the same street was the home of Charles Stewart Parnell and also the hiding place of many Fenians on the run. The street down the hill leads to the old or the Little St. George's Church which dates back to the beginning of the 18th century. This is all Luke Gardiner, Lord Mountjoy land. It was Luke who gave the site for St. George's Church, and its cemetery is off the Whitworth Road beside Drumcondra Hospital.

If you haven't seen St. George's you have missed a noble sight. Its spire can view the Royal Way or the old Mailcoach Road to Drumcondra, where you find the nicest Dublin accent, and a good drop to drink in the old Cat and Cage tavern. The spire is a comforting sight, a beautiful sight, from the barred windows of Mountjoy Jail.

Maybe Luke got his Royal Circus after all. The Jail has a circle and four grand avenues — A Wing, B Wing, C Wing, D Wing, and I don't think there is a more private residence in Dublin. Its burglar-proof from outside and inside, and if anyone calls to visit you, you can always send word to the gate to say you're always at home.

Phoenix Park

Mister! Mister! do you want any weight Mister? A chorus of voices from dozens of children standing at the Park gates, offering themselves to the lorry drivers. A nod of the head, and soon a dozen or more were hiding under the tarpaulin or empty sacks and wooden creels. As soon as the tare weight was taken, the lorry left the weighbridge scales and emptied its human cargo, paid their wages (two pence a child) and continued on to the fuel depot in The Phoenix Park. War years with ration books, a half ounce of tea and the Phoenix Park turned into a coalyard. There were turf sheds and Victory gardens became vegetable plots.

Will the Park ever be the same again? Gone too are the days of Stanley Woods and the motor-bike racing, and the Bluebird racing-car driven by a Prince. The Gough Monument never looked the same without the sandbags all around it. We never knew whether the sandbags were to protect the racing drivers or General Gough sitting up on his horse. In later years, Gough lost his sword, then his head and then he suddenly disappeared — horse, steps and all!

If you want to amuse children and at the same time have a bit of peace, take them up to the 'Monie Mount', the children's favourite name for the Wellington Testimonial in The Phoenix Park — it was raised in honour of The Duke of Wellington, the man who helped to defeat Napoleon and who was born in 24 Upper Merrion Street Dublin. Yet he claimed he was a Londoner. 'But Arthur' his friends said 'you were born in Dublin, you're a Dubliner' — the only answer he ever gave was "if I was born in a stable, it doesn't mean I'm a bloody horse". The original design for the monument was not completed due to lack of funds. What you can see today cost over £21,000, an expensive piece of playground equipment for the children of Dublin.

The Phoenix Park is really a child's paradise — the dog pond, the herd of deer, the horsemen riding, the Phoenix Pillar and the Polo grounds. You can enjoy the flower gardens or feeding the ducks or a few hours in the Zoological Gardens. Don't miss a ride on the horse train or watching seals diving for their meals, or the fifteen acres to watch the various sports and also the music in Donnelly's hollow. For the courting couples the Furry Glen, and for the old folk a seat in the shade of an elm tree, where Davis Dillon and Duffy founded the *Nation* newspaper in the year 1842. A short distance up the main road, in view of the Viceregal Lodge, Cavendish and Burke fell on the 6th May 1882. For that deed five men went to the scaffold, Joe Brady, Tim Kelly, Dan Curley, Thomas Caffrey and Michael Fagan. If you look up the road, you might see a cab driven by James FitzHarris (Skin the Goat) on his way to Green Street Courthouse and sixteen years in prison in Portlaoise Jail, rather than become

An early 19th century view of Dublin from the Phoenix Park showing Sarah's Bridge over the Liffey and the Wellington Monument. On the right horizon appears the Royal Hospital.

an informer and accept gold and pardon.

These ancient lands, robbed by Strongbow, worked by the monks of Kilmainham Priory, given to the King by John Rawson and rented to Sir Edward Fisher. Fisher built his residence on Saint Thomas' Hill now known as the Magazine Fort. Fisher exchanged the lands for land in Cornwall and the King again became the Lord and Master. Fisher's house became the home of many Viceroys including Oliver Cromwell's brother Henry. One hundred years later (1740) the house was pulled down and a Magazine Fort erected. The Viceroys moved to the King's house in Chapelizod. This house was standing up to a few years ago.

As a boy, I delivered laundry baskets to a family named Dixon who lived in the King's house — it stood beside the Church, down in a hollow. Even as a boy of thirteen years I was aware that it was an important house, it had long Queen Anne type windows, a square doorway which opened into a large square hall, beautifully furnished. I remember studying the statues of little boys and girls outside the door and in the gardens. The house and grounds still stand in my memory.

It was always our first stop every Wednesday morning on our delivery route to Leixlip Castle and the Bird's Nest [1] in Castletown House, Celbridge. That was in 1940, and I was paid two shillings and fivepence a day to tour Dublin, its neighbourhood, and to visit its historic places, houses and castles. The Viceroys later moved from the King's house to the residence in the Phoenix Park. Go up today, explore and discover the finest park in the world, let the children run around, open up your picnic basket, relax and enjoy the air. You'll find it hard to believe that you are only a few minutes' drive from the hustle and bustle of the city streets.

(1) *Bird's Nest:* The Bird's Nest Orphanage, Dun Laoghaire, moved to Castletown House, Celbridge during the last war. I think the children were transferred for fear of a bombing raid on Dun Laoghaire Port. We always delivered two laundry baskets, one marked 'Lord and Lady Carew', the other marked: 'Bird's Nest, Castletown'.

The Kings Cowboy

Liberties? Liberties be damned. We'll get Napper Tandy and he'll soon put a stop to that fellow John de Blaquiere. The cheek of him anyway, trying to make a Liberty out of the people's Phoenix Park. Ah, but he doesn't want it all — only thirty-five acres for his cows and bulls. He won't even get a paddle in the dog pond when we're finished with him. There is only one thing to do, said Napper Tandy.. We'll take him to court. I'll go now and arrange for Barry Yelverton to take our brief.

James Napper Tandy and the people
versus
Sir John Blaquiere

Blaquiere was Chief Secretary in Ireland, and in 1774 he took the post of Bailiff of the Phoenix Park, which at the time entitled him to £9 a year and a small lodge. Shortly after this he decided without permission to fence off over 30 acres of the Park near his residence. Blaquiere had no worries — his best friends were the three judges, and the jurymen were all picked for the occasion.

Not only did he win his Liberty and his land, but he was awarded £8,000 out of the taxpayers' pocket to build a new residence (now the American Legation). He later sold the lease for £7,000 even though it was supposed to belong to the Castle.

The case was held in Green Street courthouse and the three judges ruled. "It was only by leave of the King the citizens had liberty to recreate themselves under restrictions". So Blaquiere's Liberty under the Crown also gave the Crown the absolute ownership of the Phoenix Park. And now that his decision had been approved of by the courts, Blaquiere organised a salary increase of £500 per annum as payment for his side-line task as Bailiff of the Phoenix Park. He also secured unlimited grazing for his cattle in the Park.

However, Blaquiere continued to prosper and he left his name on one of our bridges — Blaquiere Bridge in Phibsboro. But this section of the Royal Canal is now gone and we have a park in its place, so no one really sees the bridge. It is there beside the State Cinema which was once called the Blaquiere Picture House. So in the words of the ballad makers in the year 1775 Blaquiere's Liberty —

Debarred the roads near our abodes
no car, nor coach shall pass,
Our cows alone (the soils our own)
Shall eat the Royal Grass.

Old Kilmainham

Sure you could write a book about it, and where will I start. A visit to the jail? The Royal Hospital? Bully's Acre? St. John's Well? Major Sirr's Stag House? The Robber's Den? Nasan Brown's Inn? or Gipsy Rose Lee's caravan home? In the sixth century, Saint Maigned built his church and gave the district its name: Cill-Maigned — the name of the church of Maigned became corrupted into Kilmainham. In 1014, on the way to Clontarf, Brian Boru rested his troops in the fields of Kilmainham. His son, Murrough, said: "If I fall in battle, take my body back here and bury me on the hilltop". Murrough fell and his grave lies today in Bully's Acre, a few yards from Emmet 's grave and the other heroes of the 1803 Rising. Emmet 's body was buried in Bully's Acre. The records state that it was taken up a week later and given to The Rev. Mr. Gamble, Saint Michan's Church. The body is not in St. Michan's vaults or churchyard. It is odd that Mr. Gamble should wait a week to claim the body, because he stood beside Emmet in his last moments. The time and place to claim the body would have been the day and hour after Emmet 's death. Why did he go to so much trouble to allow the body to be taken back to Kilmainham Jail and then be buried in Bully's Acre?This is the only graveyard that was never searched. for Emmet 's body. To prevent people from seeing the grave, they were told that the body was taken from Bully's Acre. A false entry could have been made in the records to prove this point. Denis Lambert-Redmond's last request was to be buried beside Robert Emmet — he was hanged on Wood Quay, yet his body was taken to Bully's Acre for burial. Let us search the Bully's Acre ground — who knows, the grave of Emmet might be lying in the shadows of Murrough's Cross.

The lands of Kilmainham from.the Royal Hospital gate, across to The Hole in the Wall, in the Phoenix Park and out to the home of Isolde — Princess of Dublin — in Chapelizod, were given by Strongbow to a Priory of St. John the Baptist, which was founded in the year 1174. The Order of the Hospital of St. John of Jerusalem, the fighting soldier-monks, continued in residence until they were suppressed in the 16th century.

The Duke of Ormonde became Viceroy in 1677 and between himself and King Charles II decided to erect a soldier's hospital (similar to Chelsea) in the Priory grounds. William Robinson was the architect chosen and Ormonde laid the foundation-stone on the 29th April 1680. The hospital still stands today and part of it is being prepared by the National Museum to become a folk museum. This is a place worthy of a visit and the clock-tower is one of the finest to be seen in Ireland. If the gates are locked, take a walk down John's Road and you will see the building and Bully's Acre graveyard from the road-way.

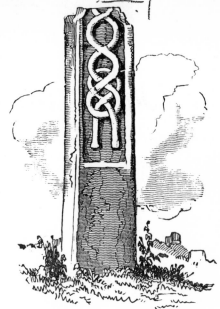

James Malton's view of the Royal Hospital in Kilmainham. This magnificent building still lies unused, even though it has been in State hands for years.
Right – a drawing of 1832 of the remains of a monument at Bully's Acre thought to mark the grave of Murrough, son of Brian who died at the battle of Clontarf.

In 1922, the last soldier pensioners were transferred from The Royal Hospital to Chelsea. During the late 1930's it was always referred to as 'the Old Man's Home'. It later became the property of The Commissioner of Police

The graves of British soldiers (who died in 1916) in Bully's Acre are kept in perpetual care, while the graves of Emmet 's men are in wilderness. Even the grave of Murrough (marked by a stone) has never been attended to. At one time, General Dilke (1760) tried to turn Bully's Acre into a botanic gardens but the men from the Liberties soon put a stop to that. They came at night-time and pulled down the walls to protect their family graves. The name Bully's Acre is a corruption of the word *bayl, baily* or *bailiff* and not from tough Dubliners as some people think.

Across the road, where the houses meet, near the Railway Bridge, stood St. John's Well, a Holy Well with curative waters where the people of Dublin came in pilgrimage on St. John's feast-day. St. John's Stations became very popular, too popular in fact, for a certain element used to mix ale and spirits with water from the Holy Well and sit there drinking it all day. Soon riots broke out and the Irish House of Commons passed an Act in 1710 threatening fines, whipping at The Royal Exchange and imprisonment for anyone found in a drunken manner at St. John's Well. This notice was posted all over Dublin and soon the drinkers stopped attending Saint John's Well. The pilgrimage was continued up to about the year 1800.

Beyond the site of Saint John's Well was Nasan Browne's Inn where Emmet and Denis Lambert Redmond had breakfast on the morning of July the 23rd, 1803. They were here to have a last look at the Artillery Barracks (Islandbridge) which was to have been attacked that evening. While they were dining, the Tavern owner, Nasan Browne, was running down Kilmainham to Dublin Castle to inform the Chief Secretary that he had seen Redmond, whom he knew was a rebel, watching the sentry on the Artillery Barracks. It was in this Barracks that John Boyle O'Reilly (the Fenian) was stationed. He was a member of the 10th Hussars and had recruited several members of the British Forces into the Fenian ranks. If you pass the gate of the Artillery Barracks and hear the sound of drums, its probably the echo of O'Reilly's Drum-Head Courtmartial. Here in the valley of two hills, facing the British War Memorial, is where Irish patriots came to plan attacks in 1803, 1867 and 1916.

The first hill, to the left, leads to Sarah Bridge and the swinging gates of the Phoenix Park. Sarah was the wife of the Duke of Westmoreland (Viceroy) and they say that the bridge was built in her name, and honour, to give her a short cut to her beloved fields in Kilmainham. The Liffey, here, is a noted place for fishing. The hill to the right takes us back by St. John's Well and Bully's Acre to Kilmainham Jail and Major Sirr's Stag House. The office of a chocolate factory stands today where the Major stood among his informers and spies. The Stag House was a type of prison where unfortunate people were held by Sirr. Many people who broke the law found themselves doing an informers job to keep within the law and get a parole (a few weeks' leave) from the Stag House and the Major's clutches. Across the road is Kilmainham Jail — where many Irish Republicans met their end. From 1797 to 1923, it was the symbol of British terror in Ireland. Go in and see the haunted cell, Anne Devlin's doorway, the Execution Yard and the Museum. See Grace Gifford's Kilmainham Madonna painted on the wall of a cell.

Gipsy Rose Lee, a colourful character who was a Romany Prince and dressed in beautiful gipsy clothes lived nearby. I can see him now standing at the corner of Lady Lane, hands on hips, head in the air and his scarlet sash blowing in the wind. The fancy fair, with its swing-boats, hoop-la stalls, ghost train and Gipsy Rose Lee telling fortunes from his caravan home. The road to the left leads to Inchicore and the road to the right goes down to Mount Brown Hill where the boundary of old Kilmainham ends, beside the cottage where Liam Mellows once lived. Mellows was executed in Mountjoy Jail, 8th of December 1922.

Kilmainham Jail and right the Courthouse which is still used. The jail was rescued from total decay by a voluntary committee who with spare-time labour restored the building and opened a museum.

The City Centre

St Stephens Green

Dublin's magnificent square, known as 'the green' has thirteen avenues radiating from it, one more than from the Arc de Triomphe in Paris. They are: South King Street, Grafton Street, Dawson Street, Kildare Street, Merrion Row Hume Street, Leeson Street, Earlsfort Terrace, Harcourt Street, Cuffe Street, Proud's Lane, York Street, Gover's Alley.

Walk up and down the thirteen avenues and if you get tired, pop into the green, feed the ducks, rent a deck chair or sit in the sun shade huts or on the wall of O'Connell Bridge. Yes, we have two O'Connell Bridges in Dublin. After your rest take a walk around the green itself, keep to the parkside among the trees and look across the road. From here you will get an excellent view of the many historic houses and buildings around the square.

Start at the corner of Grafton Street. Number three was the old Dublin Bread Company, the DBC, where Pearse and McDonagh had their morning tea and scones. Number six was the offices of The Royal Society of Antiquarians of Ireland. Their volumes and journals can be studied in the National Library and they contain a mine of information on Dublin and Ireland. The National Literary Society also met in the same house.

Number sixteen was at one time the palace of the Protestant Archbishop of Dublin. The Bishops Beresford and Magee spent a fortune on the interior decorations of this house. When Richard Whateley became Archbishop and took up residence in 1831, he threatened to whitewash the beautiful hallway and staircase. Richard didn't go down too well with the swanks of Dublin, but he was a true friend of the poor and the needy. In the evenings he used to sit on the steps of his house, smoking a long cheap clay pipe. He also played with the children of the city in the green and was never without his three mongrel dogs. For thirty-two years he was the most noted and colourful figure in Stephen's Green.

The Shelbourne Hotel stands on the site of Lord Shelbourne's residence. This gentleman was a descendant of the Fitzmaurice who came over with Strongbow and became Lord and Master in Ireland. They robbed 100,000 acres in Kerry and several thousands of acres in other counties. The Shelbournes also owned lands just outside Inchicore, and areas like Robinhood, the Fox & Geese, Blue-bell and Red Cow all belonged to his lordship. These tracts of land were all part of the manor of Drimnagh.

St. Stephen's Green

Number seventy-two was the home of 'The Sham Squire' a notorious informer of the '98 heroes. Mr. Francis Higgins got this nickname by pretending he was a relation of Lord Clonmel and married a rich merchant's daughter. He was soon found out and his new wife fled. Higgins started as a shoe-black, and later had a small huckster shop in a basement near Green Street Courthouse. He died in 1806. Oliver St. John Gogarty lived for a time in number thirty-two. St. Vincent's Hospital (old) stood on the site of Grattan's House and was the residence of the Earl of Meath. The hospital has now moved out to Elm Park and the original 18th century facade is being reproduced on part of the new site.

Iveagh House, now occupied by the Department of External Affairs, was the home of Sir Benjamin Lee Guinness "The Porter King" who saved St. Patrick's Cathedral from ruin. Watch out when you're passing number eighty-six, or the Buck Whaley might land on your back. Buck is said to have jumped from a window and landed on a passing coach. He was one of the kings of the Hell Fire Club, and for a bet of £10,000 he travelled all the way to Jerusalem, played handball on the walls of the Holy city and then made his way back again. After this he was known as Jerusalem Whaley. One of his favourite places was Daly's Club at seventeen College Green.

A strange number in St. Stephen's Green was ninety-four-and-a-half, the official number of Wesley College. The quaint old red brick building and the little chapel have gone; they stood way in off the square almost as if they were playing a game of hiding. Its sad that Wesley is no longer there, because it gave that side of the green a little bit more character and charm. Number one-hundred-and-ten was Epworth House, a residence for Wesley College girls. Number one-hundred-and-twelve is the Unitarian Church, known to generations of Dubliners as The Damer Hall, the home of actors, actresses and playwrights Some of Brendan Behan's plays first saw light of day in The Damer Hall. It is noted for plays in Gaelic. Kapp and Peterson, the famous pipe manufacturers occupied number one-hundred-and-thirteen.

The Royal College of Surgeons, is worthy of a special visit. You can gain admission to the gallery of the theatre. This is where the sack-em-ups came with the bodies stolen from graveyards. The College has a magnificent history which would fill many volumes. Sir Charles Cameron, an ex-president, wrote a book giving a detailed account of Dublin's early medical and surgical days. The College history goes back to the days of the red and white poles, when the surgeon barbers were all one body. In those days you could get a hair cut and your gallstones out at the same time, by the same doctor. Later, however, they dissected the barbers, and the only relic the barbers have today is their red and white pole. The College was taken over in 1916 by Commandant Mallin with the Countess Markievicz and The Irish Citizen Army.

A few doors away number 124 was the birthplace of Robert Emmet the darling of Erin. His statue stands opposite the College outside the green railings not far from the monument of Lord Ardilaun, the man who gave the poor of Dublin St. Stephen's Green Park.

Study the old by-laws, you can't smoke, curse, chase girls, court, bring your dog, stay after dark etc. Each gate had its own key and a person living on the green was the Key-Custodian. At one time only the gentry were allowed walk down its parks, but Lord Ardilaun changed all that. The poor of Dublin made a collection among themselves to put up the monument to this generous man.

Wesley College, now demolished to make way for part of the Russell Hotel development.

The first avenue we visit is South King Street. Here is the Gaiety Theatre, started in November 1871 by the Gunn Brothers, they also sold pianos in Grafton Street. The Gunn family kept the theatre going for many years, and it was the late Jimmy O'Dea, and Harry O'Donovan who put the Gaiety on the map of the World Theatre. The old gods (the gallery) are long gone, but can you remember the days of opera at ninepence a seat, and the singing by the audience during the interval. The famous names, great stars, the happy moments, the tears of laughter, the spotlight, the orchestral music. Jimmy O'Dea led his one-man show, until Maureen Potter came along (see chapter 'The Comedy King').

South King Street ends at the wall of Mercers Hospital, the ancient site of St. Stephen's Hospital for lepers from where the Green gets its name. St. Stephen's Hospital, founded in 1224 by the Dublin Corporation, bordered on the lands of the liberty of St. Sepulchre's (Archbishop's) and it has a chequered history. Cromwell took it over as a military barracks in 1649, and by the year 1698 the hospital, church, three castles and stone houses around it were all in ruins. A quarter of a century later Miss Mary Mercer built a house for twenty sick girls. Within a decade Mercers Hospital was established and is still today continuing the great work of care for the sick started at this site seven hundred and fifty years ago.

The second avenue is Grafton Street. Samuel Whytes Academy stood where Bewley's Shop stands today. At the corner of Chatham Street Wolfe Tone fell in love. Matilda Witherington, a beautiful sixteen-year-old, was looking out of the window of her Grafton Street home as Tone was on his way to Stephen's Green.

At the corner of South Anne Street the informer Armstrong met John and Henry Shears whom he later betrayed and sent the brothers to Newgate Gallows side-by-side. At the corner of Duke Street the Fenian, James Coady dropped his dagger while trying to kill a Fenian informer. Coady

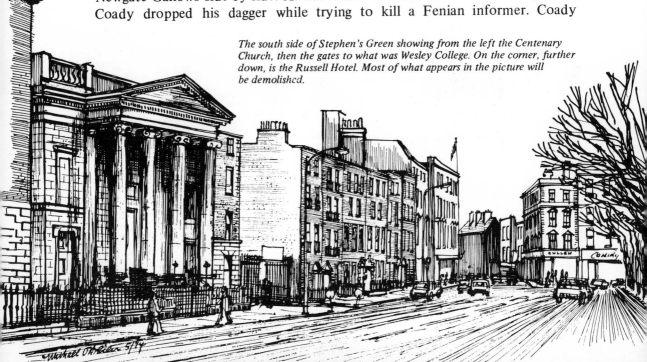

The south side of Stephen's Green showing from the left the Centenary Church, then the gates to what was Wesley College. On the corner, further down, is the Russell Hotel. Most of what appears in the picture will be demolished.

received twenty years penal servitude in an English dungeon. After his release he went to Australia and became the leader of republican opinion in support of the Irish cause. The day he dropped the dagger he ran through Johnston's Court and was arrested in Clarendon Street.

Just beyond the corner of Harry Street was McDaid's pub, the meeting-place of Brendan Behan, Patrick Kavanagh and the poets and writers of Dublin. The corner beyond McDaid's leads to Balfe Street, the birthplace of the composer, Michael Balfe, originally number 10 Pitt Street. He wrote 'The Bohemian Girl' and the immortal ballads, 'When Other Lips' and 'I dreamt I Dwelt in Marble Halls'.

The Balfe s were a very musical family and Michael learned his first notes from his father who was an accomplished violinist. Balfe's works became known all over the world and he is one of the few Dublin composers whose music and lyrics have been translated into German, French, Russian and Italian. He received many honours and was made a Chevalier of the Legion d'Honour in Paris. He died on October 20th 1869 at the age of sixty-one years. My mother's favourite musical was always 'The Bohemian Girl', but then I suppose she was clannish, she too was born in number 10 Pitt Street.

If you see a crowd of men at the corner of Wicklow Street, maybe they are on their way to The Barbers Hall at number 25 Wicklow Street. The men have urgent business, their chief James Stephens is in Richmond Jail, a new Fenian leader and military council has to be decided on. Colonel Kelly will get the chief's position, he was the man who led the raid at the smashing of the van in Manchester. The same house number 25 was also a secret meeting-place of the 1848 leaders.

The third Avenue is Dawson Street. St. Ann 's Church is where Wolfe Tone was married to the young girl from Grafton Street: St. Ann 's, noted for its lunchtime music, lectures and poetry. The parish dates from 1707 and is built on land presented by Joshua Dawson. The poet Felicia Hemans is buried in the vaults. Sir Hugh Lane, founder of the Municipal Gallery, loved St. Ann 's and might have been buried here had he not drowned at sea (sinking of *Lusitania*). The church has recently been cleaned and looks really beautiful, particularly from South Anne Street.

The Mansion House, the Lord Mayor's Residence, is noted for its round, oak and supper rooms. Here from October to Christmas sales of work, with bargains galore, book stalls, wheels of fortune, all in aid of worthy causes, are held. Horse show week brings the antique fair, where you can buy treasures of golden days, priceless objects some of which a few years ago were only junk and scrap. Prints of Dublin, books, furniture, silverware, old lamps, maps, coins, and the glitter and dust of centuries.

Number 19 is the Royal Irish Academy. Here you will find a treasure of books and where lectures and afternoon meetings are held. It has many historic associations with Dublin City. I studied a lot of Dublin's history in the Academy and had in fact made several visits before they realised I was not a member. Even when they discovered me among a mountain of Dublin books and maps they allowed me to continue, and suggested that I get a member to propose me for membership. When I saw the list of members headed by all my political enemies I decided to go back to Dean Armstrong and Marsh's Library, where I could come and go with more comfort.

Fourth Avenue is Kildare Street where Charles Dickens' son went for his two bottles of whiskey. And the drop he got from Mitchell's at number 21 was so bloody good he sat down after drinking it and wrote them a letter. That was December 24th, 1877. Charles' son also named Charles got his two bottles for thirty bob. Some of the house numbers have been altered over the years.

Number 39 was the home of Lady Morgan. It was a long journey with the jug of porter from Bridge Street. I wonder did she spill any or have a few sips on the way? Number 38 was the home of Mrs. Butler, the widow who sheltered the Fenian chief James Stephens after his escape from Richmond Jail. Stephens later went to France. Mrs. Butler went down in the world (some say due to her Fenian sympathies) and died a pauper in Ballybough.

Leinster House was originally the residence of the Fitzgerald family, the Earls of Kildare. It was Lord Edward who said "Leinster House does not inspire bright ideas". The building was started in 1745 and today it is hard to credit that a building of this scale was erected for the family. In 1815 it was sold to the RDS and later in 1922 the Irish Free State took it over. On the right of Leinster House is the National Museum, which contains a fabulous collection of Celtic and Viking ornaments, and thousands of other items. On the left facing it is our grossly overcrowded National Library, and hidden beside it, the National College of Art, once the servant quarters of Leinster House.

The Kildare Street Club has lost a lot of its dignity, and the tram conductor can no longer crack his daily joke as the tram stopped at the corner: 'Tell Carhampton I'll be late for lunch'. Here in bygone days one could find bowler hats, pin-stripes, umbrellas, walrus moustaches, "The Thin Red Line" stories of India, The Boxer Rising Victorian days, and later in Black and Tan days Sam Brown Belts, gold braid, raincoats and slouch hats, and flashing revolvers.

Between Dawson Street and Kildare Street is Molesworth Street where you will find this row of lovely 19th century buildings. On the left is the Molesworth Hall and centre 'St. Ann's School'. The present owners plan to demolish these buildings.

The Kildare Street Club after it was opened in 1861. The view is from Trinity College.

The Fifth Avenue is Merrion Row, quite short, you'll almost pass it by. Go slowly, watch for the Huguenot graveyard. The grave-stones still bear their exotic names. Raise your hat to their memory, their skills, their honest dealings. They were the French men and women who came to Dublin and found a home, and became more Dublin than Dubliners themselves. The road ahead leads to Gallows Cross at the corner of Fitzwilliam Street. It was here that Archbishop Dermot O'Hurley was hanged in 1584. He was betrayed by a man named Walter Ball, who also betrayed his own mother for sheltering the Archbishop. The area from O'Donoghue's Publichouse Merrion Row to McDaid's Publichouse in Harry Street is known to Dubliners as "The Strip". O'Donoghue's is famous for characters, ballads and booze — if you do drop in you might meet The Bishop of O'Donoghue's "Doc" — The Midnight Cowboy. This is where Ronnie Drew, Luke Kelly and the Dubliners started and where new Dublin characters are born every night.

Number 67 Baggot Street is the house where Thomas Osborne Davis died. Across the street is the house where the Shears Brothers were arrested in 1798. "If we live influenced by wind and sun and tree, and not by the passions and deeds of the past we are a thriftless and a hopeless people. From a knowledge of local history comes that permanent and proud nationality which appears to sacrifice life and wealth to liberty, but really wins all together. This country of ours is no sand-bank thrown up by some recent caprice of earth. It is an ancient land, honoured in the archives of civilisation, traceable into antiquity by its piety, its valour, and its sufferings".

Thomas Davis, Young Irelander

The east side of the Green. Some old Georgian houses on the left are joined to the newly-built building on the corner of Hume Street. This is the site of the famous 'battle of Hume Street'.

The sixth Avenue is Hume Street. Here is located the Skin and Cancer Hospital, and round the corner in Ely Place, was the home of Oliver St. John Gogarty. Could that be James Joyce I see looking out the window, he seems to be smiling, has Gogarty really given him permission to write the book? "I don't care a damn what you say of me" said Gogarty, "as long as its literature" – but then when *Ulysses* appeared in 1922 Gogarty had other words to say. "That bloody Joyce whom I kept in my youth has written a book you can read on all the lavatory walls of Dublin".

Number 4 Ely Place was also the Town Residence of John Philpot Curran. In number 6 lived Lord Clare, one of the most hated men in Ireland. Many times this house was stormed by the citizens of Dublin. Lord Clare was Attorney General in 1798 and was responsible for the execution of the rebel leaders. Ely House, where the Georgian Society meet, is today the headquarters of the Knights of Columbanus. It is one of the finest Georgian houses in Dublin and the interior hallway and staircase and ceilings are magnificent. Visitors are allowed at reasonable hours. It is said this fine building is to be demolished soon.

The seventh Avenue is Leeson Street which leads to the gateway of Dublin. This was the Royal way along which the Kings, Queens and Viceroys of England entered the city. At Leeson Street Bridge the addresses of welcome were read. Halfway up the street you will turn into Pembroke Street Upper, cast a glance at number 14, the lodging-house of Edward Duffy, Rossa's friend who was arrested here and sentenced to fifteen years in an

English dungeon. On a Sunday morning in Millbank Jail, many miles across the sea from Pembroke Street, O'Donovan Rossa heard the words, whispered in by the ventilator in his prison cell door "Duffy is Dead", "Duffy is Dead". Rossa could not sleep that night, and as he twisted and turned on his wooden plank bed, he wrote a poem in his mind for Edward Duffy. One of the verses goes like this:

The gloomy way is brightened when
We walk with those we love
The heavy-load is lightened when we
Bear and they approve
The path of life grows darker to
Me as I journey on
For the truest hearts that travelled
It are falling one by one

The eighth Avenue is Earlsfort Terrace, for many years the home of University College Dublin, the old Alexandra College, and the C.D.S. Clergy's Daughters Schools. Alexandra College was recently demolished to make way for more offices, but the school continues in new premises at Milltown. For several generations this has been terrace of education for the rich, leading out to Adelaide Road, where the Eye and Ear Hospital is sited. A Presbyterian Church frames the end of the street, and further down Adelaide Road is St. Killian's, the German Lutheran Church.

The ninth Avenue is Harcourt Street. Number 22 was the residence of Leonard MacNally, the crown informer in the days of Emmet . Numbers 15 & 16 was the home of Copper Face Jack, John Scott, Earl of Clonmel. He was the judge who tried the Rev. Mr. Jackson in the Four Courts at Christchurch. Jackson fell dead in the dock (he took his own life) but Clonmel still insisted that he be brought to his feet so that he could sentence him to death.

Next-door in number 14 lived Sir Jonah Barrington. Jonah's wife had habit of looking out the side-window into the Earl's garden. The Earl made a smart remark to Jonah about his pimping wife, Jonah was so furious that he called in a team of masons and had the window blocked up. You can still see it today in the laneway beside number 14. Jonah was a friend of the Shears Brothers and he voted against the Act of Union in 1800.

Number 6 Harcourt Street was the home of Cardinal Newman. It was also the headquarters of Sinn Fein, and if you could imagine a small man on the roof, it would be Joe Clarke, the caretaker, watching for Black and Tans to pass so that Collins, Boland and Brugha could get safely away.

Number 40 was the High School Dublin where George Bernard Shaw got his early education. This school is still with us but has moved out of town. It was founded by Erasmus Smith. The beautiful railway station which once provided the terminal for the Bray via Dundrum line is now used as offices. The Old Court Laundry which stood nearby is gone. Do you remember the lovely laundry vans painted primrose and white with their well groomed horses, polished brasses and black oiled leather harness. Many a year they made their way to the R.D.S. Horse Show to collect winners ribbons and cups. My old van in the White Heather was always like a tramp beside them. One day I remarked on this to my van man. He snarled at me and said "We don't go in for washing vans, we go in for washing clothes". Nevertheless, the Court Laundry vans added glamour and dignity to the streets of Dublin.

The tenth Avenue is Cuffe Street. The house I miss most is Mr. Coppolo's Ice Cream Parlour. He was the King of Ice Cream in Dublin. Some people made ice cream from sweetened tin milk and water and it tasted like cornflour. Coppolo's ice cream (Lord rest him) had a flavour I couldn't describe. It was only gorgeous — wafers as thick as your head for a penny.

This small street at one time had four pawn shops. One of them was in the back kitchen of number 47. Dean Walter Blake Kirwan, the Jesuit who went over to the other side lived here. He was a powerful preacher and when he gave a charity sermon the ladies and gents filled the plates with their gold rings, jewellery, tie pins, cuff-links etc. Some of this was only given for show. The next day they would call to Cuffe Street to redeem the object for a few shillings, saying that it fell into the plate in error. Today only one pawnbroker's shop remains. It is Gormans which is number 48. It stands next-door to 'The Bricklayers' Hall', which is a fine example of stonework. Alas, both are soon to be demolished.

The pawnshop in number 48 Cuffe Street was previously named Meredith & Co. It was owned by a Mr. Edward Sheridan of Sandymount in 1917. Next-door (49) is the headquarters of the Ancient Guild of Incorporated Brick and Stonelayers Trade Unions, which is one of the oldest Guilds in Dublin This Guild has a long and coloured history and caused a stoppage of work on Gandon's Custom House (1795) in protest against stone-masons being brought over from England. This was a time that Dublin was full of stone and brick craftsmen.

Stone-laying in bygone days was a fine art job, as can be seen by the old walls at St. Audoen's, Christchurch and Dublin Castle.

Cuffe Street was also a meeting place for the Irish Invincibles in 1882.

The eleventh Avenue is Proud's Lane. Can you see two men in green and grey uniforms with short mauser rifles looking into the yard of Beverley Smith's to see if they can commandeer the large furniture removal vans to use as a barricade? This happened during the 1916 Rising.

The twelfth Avenue is York Street, where Clarence Mangan worked as a clerk to a solicitor. He later lived for a time at number 6. Mangan fell in love with a married woman, Margaret Stackpoole from Ranelagh. She never told Mangan she was married, but just led him on to the day he bought the ring. After she let him propose, she then told him. Mangan went home to write "The Nameless One" and then took to the drink. He later contracted fever and was found dying in a cellar in Bride Street. He died in the Meath Hospital in

1849.

The best-known house in York Street was number 41, "The Workmans Club". The Dublin Total Abstinence League, whose motto was 'Ireland Sober Ireland Free' the people about whom Brendan Behan said "would only speak Irish but wouldn't drink Irish". It was a mecca of I.R.A. men in Black and Tan days. The Christmas Draws provided great excitement, only threepence a ticket and nearly one hundred prizes — turkeys, hampers, wine, cakes and five-pound notes. The best value in raffle tickets at Christmas was always "The Workmans Club". "Keep me two Missus, I'll see ya Saturday, don't let them go now, Saturday". Many a poor family dined like kings on a Christmas Day, thanks to the Workmans Club. The ticket itself was worth the threepence. A large piece of coloured paper with a serial number in the top corner and every prize listed. Also included were the closing date, day of draw, newspaper notice and the latest time to claim your winnings.

A building very much in use in York Street today is the Salvation Army Men's Hostel. Here a man can find a bed for the night, sit and relax in the television room and also enjoy a meal in the restaurant, and all at modest prices. Most of the buildings in this street have been demolished recently, but the Salvation Army continue their long tradition here, and at their other centres around the city. The 'Sally Anne' as the Dubliners called them were always held in very high esteem in Dublin.

The thirteenth Avenue is Glovers Alley which runs along the side of the College of Surgeons. It was often used by Robert Emmet on his way home from school. In 1917 the gentry came here to make use of the Turkish Baths which stood between two mineral water manufacturing companies. They were, Hovenden Orr and Irish Direct Trading Company. At the end of the alley is the factory of Smith and Sheppard, the old established firm who manufacture artificial limbs and surgical instruments. Fannin & Co. in nearby Grafton Street are also a very old established company in the same business. It is nice to remember that Dublin manufacturers were experts in this type of work in the early days of surgical aids. And so we end our tour of the green and its thirteen avenues.

The main entrance to the Salvation Army's Hostel in York Street.

127

Trinity College

On my first day at work in Switzer's of Grafton Street, I was sent with a parcel to Trinity College. I came out of the laneway into Wicklow Street and started to walk up towards George's Street. It suddenly dawned on me that I didn't know where Trinity College was. Near the top of Exchequer Street I asked a policeman. He sent me down Dame Court and told me to turn right and that it was the large building stretching across the street. He also shouted after me that there were two statues in front of it looking out and another statue looking in. As I came closer to The College, I examined the address label and wondered what was inside. "With care – Fragile: Mr. T. L. Wilkins, Junior Fellow, T.C.D." Then I began to notice The College, the small window panes, the pillars, the way it stood in the centre of the street, the clock and flag-pole; then I started counting the windows – 43, 44, 45; then I bumped into a lamp-post!

I stood at the statue of Grattan and gazed like a tourist – another gaze at Burke and Goldsmith before getting in by the open wicket door in the arch-type gateway. The gateman sat in his little office on the left. His desk was filled with papers, books, wire clips and dozens of door keys. He was dressed in a navy blue swallow-tail coat and a black cap like those I saw in Tyson's window. He examined the label and gave me directions. As I went through the dark, dimly-lit hallway, I saw the scores of notices: "Lost and Found"; "Room Wanted"; "Divinity Books for Sale"; "Meeting Tonight"; "Dance in the Boat Club" and a thought for the day – "Very few of us get dizzy from doing good turns". I could have stopped there all day reading. I crossed the cobblestone Parliament Square, peeped into the Chapel and the Examination Hall and gave the same attention and gaze to The Campanile as I had done to Grattan outside the gate.

I could see the rows of books behind the Library window and now and again a face appeared. Another black-capped swallow-tail-coated man passed me by, and then I saw an elderly grey-haired Clergyman who looked rather odd in his light-brown buttoned gaiters, his black-thorned walking stick with a silver top, and a thick gold watch-chain across his green-coloured waistcoat. The Clergyman suddenly called out: 'skip, skip' – I thought he was talking to me. 'Beg your pardon sir', I said. "The skip, the skip" he said, pointing after the man in the black cap. I put my fingers into my mouth and gave a loud whistle which echoed all over the quiet College grounds. The skip turned and noticed the waving blackthorn stick and came running back. By the look on his face, I think he thought the Clergyman had given the whistle signal. The old 'skip' tradition in Trinity died when the last one was buried recently. I moved along fast and found the address I was looking for.

On my way back out, I read a few more notices in the hallway, gave the gateman a 'thank you' salute which he returned with a smile and I gave another salute to Grattan which he didn't return at all! That was the first of a thousand parcels I delivered to Trinity College, to the Provost's house, the G.M.B. (Graduate Memorial Building), the School of Divinity, the Senior Fellows, the Junior Fellows and a few students who were called Junior and Senior Freshmen and Junior and Senior Sophister.

I can recall the College rag-days when the students dressed up in all sorts of gear and some with hardly any gear! kissing girls, letting the air out of bicycle wheels, stopping trams and motors, doing point-duty in a pair of pyjamas. They held parades with floats through the streets of Dublin City, and carried on with every type of behaviour that was unbecoming of Trinity boys. The Provost put down his boot and the rag days were banned. Despite the behaviour of the students, the Dublin people loved the rag days and the money collected always went to a deserving charity.

The Archbishop of Dublin, Adam Loftus, was the man responsible for getting the Charter from Queen Elizabeth and the land from the Lord Mayor, and the people of Dublin. In fact the Lord Mayor, Thomas Smith, laid the

Trinity College facing College Green.

foundation-stone on the 13th of April, 1591, and the College doors opened for students on the 9th of January, 1593. For almost four hundred years, the College has been the principal University of the Nation. Dean Swift, Edmund Burke, Oliver Goldsmith, Grattan, Tone, Emmet, Moore, Davis and a host of other famous names passed through its gateway since then. The name on the Royal Charter read:

> " The Provost, Fellows and Scholars of the Holy
> and Undivided Trinity of Queen Elizabeth
> near Dublin."

The College site was originally the old Augustinian Monastery of All Hallows or All Saints, which was built in 1166 by Dermot Mac Murrough— King of Leinster. The dissolved monastery of All Hallows was granted to the citizens of Dublin in 1534 for their loyal support and losses sustained during the Rebellion of Silken Thomas, son of the Earl of Kildare.

The greatest treasure of the College is The Book of Kells, often referred to as the most beautified testimony to Christian faith. It can be seen in the Old Library under its armour plate glass. In 1953 the Book of Kells was bound into four volumes for greater protection for the generations unborn. Every year, more than a quarter of a million people from all over the world visit the Library. The Book of Kells is the work of the monks of Saint Columba, who was an Irish Saint who went to Iona in A.D.563 with twelve followers and converted half of Scotland and Northern England to Christianity. Early in the ninth century, the followers of Saint Columba decided to produce a book more beautiful than any other. The skins of one hundred and fifty calves produced the smooth vellum leaves. The colours used by the illuminators came from plants and flowers. Four chief artists, assisted by several other monks, spent a lifetime with their labour of love.

In 806, the Vikings raided Iona and killed sixty eight monks at Martyr's Bay. During the raid, the artist monks escaped with their book and came across the sea to Ireland and were given refuge at Kells, Co. Meath. Here, the book was completed and remained on display in Kells for nearly two-hundred years. The Annals of Ulster record: "The chief relic of The Western World was wickedly stolen in the night in the year 1006". The thieves buried the book and it was discovered a few months later. In the 12th century, the book was in the care of the Bishop of Meath where it was venerated as the great Gospel Book of St. Columba. Henry Jones, Scoutmaster-General to Cromwell, became Bishop of Meath in 1661 and he presented The Book of Kells to Trinity College Library.

Other treasures in the College are: The Book of Durrow, The Book of Armagh, The Garland of Howth, The Book of Leinster, the Spanish Organ, the Brian Boru Harp and thousands of rare, priceless antiquarian books in the Library. Under The Copyright Act, Trinity get a free copy of every book published in Ireland and Britain.

Looking across Parliament Square at the Chapel of Trinity College.

King James II used the College as a Military Barracks in 1689. James appointed the only Catholic Provost it ever had, the Rev. Father Michael Moore. Trinity was the first College to grant Degrees to Jews and confer degrees on women. In the years 1724-1855 Professors of Language and Literature taught Greek, Latin, English, Irish, German, Hebrew, Arabic, Persian, Hindustani and Romantic languages.

In the year 1785, Francis Andrews, Provost, endowed The Astronomical Observatory at Dunsink, Castleknock, which was placed by Statute in 1791 under the management of the Royal Astronomer of Ireland. The Ballast Office Clock, at Westmoreland Street (the one that's always right according to Dubliners!) was controlled by an electric current transmitted each second by a time-clock in the Observatory. A few clocks in Trinity College were also controlled by the same system.

The West Front Building dates from 1752 and was designed by Keane and Sanderson. In 1759, the Provost's House was built by an Irish Architect, John Smyth, who copied, and changed in parts, Lord Burlington's design of a London house. The Chapel was designed by Sir William Chambers in 1787, and cost £22,000 to build. The Campanile, which replaced the old Belfry, was the gift of the Primate, Lord George Beresford in 1852. Trinity College stretches from the front gate at College Green to the back gate at Lincoln Place, near Westland Row, where Synge, the playwright was born. Trinity is really a city within a city. As each day passes new buildings and extensions continue. Students come from all over the world to study at The University of Dublin. James Joyce said that Trinity was a dull stone. I beg to differ, Mr. Joyce, Trinity is one of the brightest jewels in the City of Dublin!

Around College Green

'Excuse me Sir,' the gentle voice said, 'could you show us the way to the old Irish Parliament House'. I turned around and saw a group of teenage girls. Tourists, no doubt, with rucksacks, tin mugs, kettles, black boots, coloured jeans and heavy woollen jumpers. Blondes, brunettes and even a red-head, all smiling, with maps and brochures in their hands. The gentle voice told me that I was in the company of New Zealand schoolteachers who were on a tour of Europe. This was their first visit to Dublin. I couldn't resist the the temptation to give an instant tour!

'I'll take you there myself', I said, and suddenly I was surrounded by the pretty group. The maps and brochures were stuck into rucksacks and out came the notebooks and pens; "spell that please, what date did you say, what street is that?" "That's D'Olier Street, a good Huguenot name, a Sherriff of Dublin." "Did you ever hear of Samuel Lover, the writer and artist? Well he lived in No. 9 D'Olier Street. He's the man who wrote the story of Rory O'Moore, the leader of the 1641 Rising. The battle-cry in those days was: 'For God, Ireland and Rory O'Moore'." "Where's the Red Bank Res-taurant?" one girl asked. "Beside you", I said, "but they don't serve food today, they serve Mass instead — its the Chapel of The Blessed Sacrament Fathers". I don't think that they were all R.C's but in they went to light candles and say a quiet prayer. As I stood in the porchway, I wondered what Joyce or Gogarty would say, if they could see the shrines and pews on the floor of the Red Bank.

We walked across by Fleet Street, the birthplace of Kevin Barry. They had heard the ballad and one of them hummed it quietly as we passed The Irish Times — the oldest daily newspaper in Ireland, founded in 1859. I told them the story of old Mr. Smylie who refused to print his paper with the new fangle machine and stuck to the old method for many years because he did not wish to make a large number of type-setters redundant. I told them, also, of The Sinn Fein Rebellion Handbook that The Irish Times printed after the 1916 Rising — it cost one shilling and sixpence then. Today its £5 or more in the secondhand bookshops of Dublin. They say in Dublin "If you miss the Irish Times, you miss part of the day and if you go into The Pearl Bar, you'll miss the whole bloody day!" The Pearl was the writer's paradise where you could find Roddy the Rover, Myles na Gopaleen, James Plunkett, Brendan Behan and Patrick Kavanagh looking for 'wan lousy word' to finish his poem. It was the boozing place of journalists, copy-boys, compositors, actors and artists.

'Come across the street, girls', I said 'and view the Parliament in three dimensions, the Ionic columns were designed by Edward Lovett Pearse who died before his beautiful building was completed. Around the corner, the Corinthian Pillars were designed by James Gandon and The Foster Place Pillars were designed by Robert Parke.' We stood at the statue of Thomas Osborne Davis and the girls giggled at the Omo suds and bubbles in the fountain waters beside the statue. 'The students', I said 'and its not even a rag-day'.

Parliament House is today The Bank of Ireland, who moved from Mary's Abbey in 1803. For £40,000 they purchased the finest building of its kind in the world. Perhaps it was sold to a Bank to prevent others from making political speeches in its chambers. Maybe they were afraid that the golden words spoken against the Act of Union of 1800 still lingered around the Waterford glass chandelier in the House of Lords, and that the spirit of the words would inspire others to re-establish the Independent Parliament. The windowless building is adorned by the statues of Wisdom, Justice and Liberty, designed by Edward Smyth.

Sir Arthur Chichester, Cromwell's man who planned the Plantation of Ulster, leased his house to The Irish Parliament in 1661. The present building was started in 1729. The Westmoreland Street front dates from 1785 and the Foster Place front from 1787. The total cost was more than £95,000. Foster Place gets its name from John Foster, the last speaker in the old Irish Parliament or 'Grattan's Parliament' as some historians call it. The Bank porter told us that his uniform of red, blue and yellow was the same colour as the colours worn by the Parliament staff in days gone by. He showed us King William crossing the Boyne and the Siege of Derry woven in beautiful wall-length tapestries, the silver mace of the House of Commons, the glass chandelier and the wood-carved mantlepiece and told us interesting tales of Daly's Club, Jonah Barrington, the duels and the fire-eaters of Dublin who used the statue of St. Andrew as a cock-shot in target shooting practise.

Looking towards the Bank of Ireland from College Street. The controversial Central Bank building appears behind. On the left are the railings of Trinity College.

College Green with the statue of Grattan and the Ulster Bank.

The statue stands today, hidden in the yard of St. Andrew's Church in Suffolk Street. The New Zealand girls desired to see it and within a few moments, we were making our way up Church Lane. I told them that St. Andrew's stood on ancient land at one time named the Thingmote, a mount or hill over the town of Dublin where laws were made and robbers hanged, and Adam O'Toole burned at the stake in the year 1327 for daring to say that the Book of Gospels was only fables. We looked for Vanessa's grave in the churchyard but looked in vain. We cleaned the tombstones with our hands to read the names, but Vanessa Vanhomrigh was not among them. I told them the story of how Vanessa died, with a broken heart in Turnstile Alley, beside Foster Place and how Stella reared Vanessa's child.

Vanessa was a girl in the life of Dean Swift — a jealous girl who heard of Swift and Stella. She wrote a letter to Stella and spoke of her love for the Dean, and asking many pertinent questions. Stella showed the letter to Swift. Mad with rage, he rode to Celbridge where Vanessa was staying, burst in the door, threw down the letter, cursed and raved, cursed and raved again and again, until Vanessa fell in a hysterical and violent manner. For many days, she lay in agony, she would not eat, she would not drink, but wept bitter tears for her loneliness, her foolishness and her unreturned love. She came back to her city residence, broken in health, rejected in love with nothing to live for, not even her child, who was now in other hands. She died of a broken heart and her grave lies under the roadway beside McCullough-Pigott's in Suffolk Street.

St. Andrew's Church, which dates from the eleventh century, was originally in Palace Street beside Dublin Castle. In 1670 the Thingmote was levelled and a church built. In 1690 it was used as a prison. The present church, built in 1866, was designed by Lanyon, Lynn and Lanyon of Belfast. St. Andrew's is the only Protestant Church in Dublin with a statue of its patron outside its door. I concluded by saying that St. Andrew's was the parish church of the old Irish Parliament House, and there I left my new-found friends from New Zealand. As I walked away, I heard their cameras clicking around St. Andrew's Church, its bullet-scarred statue and at the centre of the street, the uninscribed tomb of Vanessa Vanhomrigh.

134

Dublins Revolutionary Square

The Rotunda Hospital, previously known as The Lying-in Hospital, is the oldest and the first maternity hospital in the world. From this revolutionary venture in medicine and hospitalisation, involving pre- and post-natal care, came other revolutionary ideas and methods which first saw the light of day beside the Rotunda and around its beautiful Square (Parnell Square).

This is the 'Square of the Firsts'. Let's walk around it and you will see what I mean. The Rotunda Hospital was founded in 1757 by Dr. Bartholomew Mosse who was the fifth son of the Rector of Maryborough (Portlaoise) and was born a few hundred yards from where this is being written. Dr. Mosse had a very colourful career and visited several European cities. He returned to Dublin in 1742 and opened his first hospital in George's Lane in 1745 (opposite Fade Street) in an old disused theatre. From a small start of six beds, the hospital grew. He continued to convince his friends that the lack of "lying-in hospitals" was the prime cause of the high death rate in maternity cases.

Soon his idea became the fad of the rich and as funds poured in Mosse acquired the site on which the hospital stands today. His life was spent in the service of the poor of Dublin. It was his idea to erect the Round Rooms, and Assembly Hall, where The Ambassador Cinema, The Gate Theatre and The Town and Country Club stand today. His plan was that the funds raised from functions, meetings, balls and so on, would pay for the upkeep of his hospital.

The Rotunda Hospital was designed by the architect Richard Cassells, and was completed following the death of Cassells, by his assistant John Ensor. Dr. Mosse died before the Round and Assembly Rooms were erected but his idea was continued by his successor, Sir Fielding Ould.

Now you don't have to be expecting a baby to go in and visit The Rotunda. Push in the hall-door (at reasonable hours), climb the beautiful staircase designed by Robert West and the door facing you at the top of the stairs leads to The Rotunda Chapel. This chapel is a real gem of Dublin. The plaster-work was carried out by a Frenchman, Bartholomew Carmillion, who came to Dublin and left behind him a masterpiece for generations of Dubliners to admire. Others of his kind came also and together with Irish and Dublin craftsmen left us a heritage in Dublin to admire and wonder at. Names like Bossi, Adams, Thorpe, Stapleton, West, Kaufman and the Francini Brothers. Read C. P. Curran's book "Dublin Decorative Plasterwork", its a treasure in words and pictures.

The Rotunda Round Rooms, now the Ambassador, was the birthplace of the Irish Volunteers. It was also used by Napper Tandy and the United

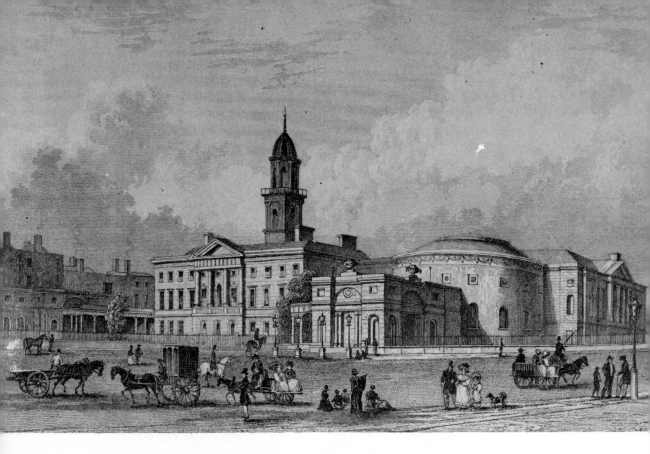

This beautiful engraving illustrates how the Rotunda Hospital and Assembly Rooms looked when completed. Today the Ambassador Cinema and Gate Theatre occupy the buildings on the right, but the hospital continues in its great tradition.

Irishmen in 1796. From that date onwards it was the meeting-place of the revolutionaries of 1848, 1867, 1882 up to the birth of the Sinn Fein organisation on 28th November 1905. Eight years later a new generation founded another Irish Volunteer Movement that led to the 1916 Easter Week Rising. The first lecture on Socialism and the Irish People by Robert Owens was also delivered here.

Across the street was Tom Clarke's shop on the corner of Parnell Street and O'Connell Street. Tom Clarke's was the first signature on the Proclamation of 1916. Just beyond the Hospital at the top of Moore Street — Padraig Pearse, the first President of the Provisional Irish Republic, handed over his sword in surrender to General Lowe of the British Forces. As the surrender order by Pearse and Connolly was obeyed, the first prisoners laid down their arms and weapons at the Parnell Monument and spent their first night in the open prison of the Rotunda gardens in front of the hospital's main door.

The Gate Theatre, the brainchild of Lord and Lady Longford, is not the same since Lord Longford passed on — the gracious Lady added dignity to the Square as she stood with her collection-box between the two large queues. "House Full" for the cinema, "House Full" for the dance hall, and Lady Longford was aware that her Gate Theatre was half empty. She always had a special row of seats – the back row – costing only a shilling a seat for the hard-up people who wished to enjoy a night at the theatre. Micheál MacLiammóir and Hilton Edwards are still with The Gate, and they have added greatly to the theatrical history of Dublin.

As we go around the Square we will call to mind the memories of Richard Kirwan who lived in No.6 Cavendish Row. Richard was "The Philosopher of Dublin" in the year 1787, and was a member of the Royal Irish Academy and the Royal Dublin Society. His works came under the subjects of Divinity, Logic, Law, Chemistry, Geology, Metaphysics, Mining and several other scientific matters. He was involved in the publication of many books and helped Bunting in his collection of Irish music. He was also the first man in Dublin to offer a reward to his servants for catching flies. He only shaved on a Thursday, the day he allowed ladies to visit him– if anyone overstayed their welcome Richard would leave the room and when he came back **he** was dressed in his pyjamas and nightcap, with a candle-holder in his hand.

Groome's Hotel was the site of the old Hay Hotel. It got its name from the fact that one of the windows in the hotel was always open with a supply of hay for the jarvey and coachmen's horses, while the gentlemen wined and dined. The Hay Hotel provided a 24 hour service.

Number 5 Parnell Square was once the home of Oliver St. John Gogarty. He was the first man to capture "the Dublin idiom" – its slang, manners and expressions in his play "Blight"; several years before Joyce and O'Casey had written their works. Number 9 was the headquarters of Sinn Fein for many years as was Number 16. Number 10 was the Grand Orange Hall of Ireland in 1917. Its a pity that these two neighbours did not make friends during that period. If they had I'm certain that Ireland today would be a far better and happier country than it is now.

The turn to the right at Chawkey's Restaurant leads to three hotels – The Castle, Barry's and The Belvedere, which is opposite Joyce's School, Belvedere College. This is a part of Dublin that feeds half of the country on All Ireland Day at Croke Park.

The Abbey Presbyterian Church known as Findlater's Church always has a warm welcome for visitors. It was built in 1864 at the expense of Alexander Findlater, the founder of Dublin's famous Grocery, Wine & Spirits shops. Twenty years ago a fleet of Findlater's lorries delivered all over Ireland, and O'Connell Street lost a bit of its character when the firm closed down a few years ago. The Technical School beside the church was once the home of Annie Hutton, the sweetheart of Thomas Davis, the Young Ireland Leader who died in 1845 a few weeks before his wedding day. Their love remains immortal in Davis's ballad "Annie Dear".

Number 20 houses The Banba Hall (National Ballroom) and The Irish National Union of Vintners, Grocers and Allied Trades' Assistants. This Union has a proud record of association with the fight for independence. Many of its members made the supreme sacrifice on the scaffold and in the streets of Dublin, the most noted name being Martin Savage who was killed in action during the Black and Tan War on the Ashtown Road. Next door — The Municipal Art Gallery, the first of its kind in Europe was the town house of John Caulfield, the Earl of Charlemont. The Earl was the Commander-in-Chief of the Volunteers of 1782. Charlemont House dates from 1763 — It was designed by Sir William Chambers on the site known as Palace Row. The Earl had his country residence at The Casino, Marino, in Dublin.

The Art Gallery has a wonderful collection of modern art. Go in and see half of Hugh Lane's collection. The other half is in a London gallery. Lane's last wish was for the full collection to remain in Dublin and he added a codicil to this effect. After he was drowned, when *The Lusitania* sank, it was discovered that the codicil on his will had no witness, and his collection of paintings at that time (1915) were on loan to a London gallery. The British refused to hand over the collection. After many years of verbal battle it was agreed (which was against the last wishes of Lane) that the collection be divided and exchanged every five years. When you visit the Gallery seek out Corot's Landscape with three figures, which they say was painted on his death-bed.

Across the Square behind the iron railings stand another three figures, Oisin Kelly's beautiful 'Children of Lir' changing into swans, erected recently in commemoration of many of those who died in the long fight for independence.

Number 24 was the office of a newspaper 'An Claidheann Soluis' organ of The Gaelic League. Colaiste Mhuire stands today on the site of Number 25 — the old headquarters of The Gaelic League, where the final plans for Easter Week were first discussed. The turn to the right leads to Granby Lane where Matt Talbot dropped dead on his way to mass in Dominick Street Friary.

The Black Church up the hill across Dorset Street, calls to mind the recent death of the great Dublin poet Austin Clarke, whose book *'Twice Around The Black Church'* is another gem of Dublin city. Revolutionary Square — yes indeed — Vaughan's Hotel at Number 29, scene of Black and Tan raids and I.R.A. escapes and arrests. Number 31 is the home of the A.O.H., or their full title The Board of the Ancient Order of Hibernians Registered Friendly Society who tried to take support from the Irish Volunteers in 1913, and yet when the Easter Rising started some of the Hibernian Rifles were side-by-side with the rebels.

Number 41 housed The Irish National Foresters, and Number 44 the headquarters of The National Volunteers. Look at its doorway which opened 'and shut on thousands of Irish Republican Revolutionaries from the days of Pearse. To-day it provides the headquarters for *An Phoblacht* the Republican newspaper. Inside there is also a shop which sells all kinds of craft souvenirs and hand-made goods, many of which are made by Republican prisoners in jails and internment camps. Joe Clarke, the 1916 veteran is often to be found here. He took part in the famous Battle of Mount Street Bridge which was one of the fiercest battles of the 1916 Rising. Joe Clarke has been an activist all his life and was the caretaker of the old Sinn Fein Headquarters in Harcourt Street, the courier of the First Dail Eireann (January 21st 1919) and the publisher of the *Wolfe Tone Weekly*. He spent several terms in jail and is probably the oldest active Revolutionary in the world.

Yes, the Square is a far cry from the days when each house provided a town residence for the gentry and nobility, yet many of the elegant doorways and some ornamental plasterwork remain to remind us of those far off days.

Looking up Parnell Street towards the Parnell Monument
the tower of the Rotunda Hospital dominates the skyline.

Index

141